Business Tax FA 2020

Level 4
Professional Diploma
in Accounting

Question Bank

For assessments from
January to December 2021

Fifth edition 2020

ISBN 9781 5097 3455 9

British Library Cataloguing-in-Publication Data

A catalogue record for this book is available from the British Library

Published by

BPP Learning Media Ltd
BPP House, Aldine Place
142-144 Uxbridge Road
London W12 8AA

www.bpp.com/learningmedia

Printed in the United Kingdom

> Your learning materials, published by BPP Learning Media Ltd, are printed on paper obtained from traceable sustainable sources.

The contents of this book are intended as a guide and not for professional advice. Although every effort has been made to ensure that the contents of this book are correct at the time of going to press, BPP Learning Media makes no warranty that the information in this book is accurate or complete and accepts no liability for any loss or damage suffered by any person acting or refraining from acting as a result of the material in this book.

We are grateful to the AAT for permission to reproduce the practice assessment(s). The answers to the practice assessment(s) have been published by the AAT. All other answers have been prepared by BPP Learning Media Ltd.

Contents

			Page
Introduction			iv

Question and answer bank

Chapter tasks		Questions	Answers
Chapter 1	Tax framework	3	73
Chapter 2	Computing trading income	6	76
Chapter 3	Capital allowances	15	81
Chapter 4	Computing corporation tax	24	88
Chapter 5	Taxing unincorporated businesses	30	91
Chapter 6	Partnerships	34	96
Chapter 7	National insurance	39	100
Chapter 8	Losses	41	104
Chapter 9	Self assessment for individuals	47	108
Chapter 10	Self assessment for companies	50	110
Chapter 11	Chargeable gains – the basics	53	113
Chapter 12	Further aspects of chargeable gains	58	119
Chapter 13	Share disposals	61	123
Chapter 14	Reliefs for chargeable gains	66	128
AAT AQ2016 practice assessment 1		135	
AAT AQ2016 practice assessment 2		137	
BPP practice assessment 1		141	159
BPP practice assessment 2		171	187
BPP practice assessment 3		199	217
BPP practice assessment 4		229	243
Tax reference material FA 2020		251	

Introduction

This is BPP Learning Media's AAT Question Bank for *Business Tax*. It is part of a suite of ground-breaking resources produced by BPP Learning Media for AAT assessments.

This Question Bank has been written in conjunction with the BPP Course Book, and has been carefully designed to enable students to practise all of the learning outcomes and assessment criteria for the units that make up *Business Tax*. It is fully up to date as at August 2020 and reflects both the AAT's qualification specification and the sample assessment provided by the AAT.

This Question Bank contains tasks corresponding to each chapter of the Course Book. Some tasks are designed for learning purposes, others are of assessment standard.

The emphasis in all tasks and assessments is on the practical application of the skills acquired.

Assessments up to 31 December 2021 will use the rules contained in Finance Act 2020 so tasks will focus on tax rates and thresholds for the tax year 2020/21 and financial year 2020. It may be that you have to deal with other tax years at work, in which case the rates and thresholds you use will be different. This Question Bank is focused on your assessment up to 31 December 2021.

VAT

You may find tasks throughout this Question Bank that need you to calculate or be aware of a rate of VAT. This is stated at 20% in these examples and questions.

Approaching the assessment

When you sit the assessment it is very important that you follow the on screen instructions. This means you need to carefully read the instructions, both on the introduction screens and during specific tasks.

When you access the assessment you should be presented with an introductory screen with information similar to that shown below (taken from the introductory screen from one of the AAT's AQ2016 sample assessments for *Business Tax*).

We have provided this **sample assessment** to help you familiarise yourself with our e-assessment environment. It is designed to demonstrate as many of the question types that you may find in a live assessment as possible. It is not designed to be used on its own to determine whether you are ready for a live assessment.

At the end of this sample assessment you will receive an immediate result. This will **not** take into account your response to tasks 3, 4, 9 and 11. In the live assessment these tasks will be human marked so you will not receive an immediate result.

Assessment information:

You have **2 hours** to complete this sample assessment.

This assessment contains **11 tasks** and you should attempt to complete every task.
Each task is independent. You will not need to refer to your answers in previous tasks.
Read every task carefully to make sure you understand what is required.

Task 9 requires extended writing as part of your response to the questions. You should make sure you allow adequate time to complete this task.

Where the date is relevant, it is given in the task data.

You may use minus signs or brackets to indicate negative numbers **unless** task instructions say otherwise.

You must use a full stop to indicate a decimal point.
For example, write 100.57 NOT 100,57 or 100 57

You may use a comma to indicate a number in the thousands, but you don't have to.
For example, 10000 and 10,000 are both acceptable.

If rounding is required, normal mathematical rounding rules should be applied **unless** task instructions say otherwise.

The actual instructions will vary depending on the subject you are studying for. It is very important you read the instructions on the introductory screen and apply them in the assessment. You don't want to lose marks when you know the correct answer just because you have not entered it in the right format.

In general, the rules set out in the AAT practice assessments for the subject you are studying for will apply in the real assessment, but you should carefully read the information on this screen again in the real assessment, just to make sure. This screen may also confirm the VAT rate used if applicable.

A full stop is needed to indicate a decimal point. We would recommend using minus signs to indicate negative numbers and leaving out the comma signs to indicate thousands, as this results in a lower number of key strokes and less margin for error when working under time pressure. Having said that, you can use

whatever is easiest for you as long as you operate within the rules set out for your particular assessment.

You have to show competence throughout the assessment and you should therefore complete all of the tasks. Don't leave questions unanswered.

In some assessments, written or complex tasks may be human marked. In this case you are given a blank space or table to enter your answer into. You are told in the assessments which tasks these are (**Note.** There may be none if all answers are marked by the computer).

If these involve calculations, it is a good idea to decide in advance how you are going to lay out your answers to such tasks by practising answering them on a word document or excel spreadsheet, and certainly you should try all such tasks in this Question Bank and in the AAT's environment using the sample assessment.

When asked to fill in tables, or gaps, never leave any blank even if you are unsure of the answer. Fill in your best estimate.

Note that for some assessments where there is a lot of scenario information or tables of data provided (eg tax tables), you may need to access these via 'pop-ups'. Instructions will be provided on how you can bring up the necessary data during the assessment.

Finally, take note of any task specific instructions once you are in the assessment. For example you may be asked to enter a date in a certain format or to enter a number to a certain number of decimal places.

Grading

To achieve the qualification and to be awarded a grade, you must pass all the mandatory unit assessments, all optional unit assessments (where applicable) and the synoptic assessment.

The AAT Level 4 Professional Diploma in Accounting will be awarded a grade. This grade will be based on performance across the qualification. Unit assessments and synoptic assessments are not individually graded. These assessments are given a mark that is used in calculating the overall grade.

How overall grade is determined

You will be awarded an overall qualification grade (Distinction, Merit, and Pass). If you do not achieve the qualification you will not receive a qualification certificate, and the grade will be shown as unclassified.

The marks of each assessment will be converted into a percentage mark and rounded up or down to the nearest whole number. This percentage mark is then weighted according to the weighting of the unit assessment or synoptic assessment within the qualification. The resulting weighted assessment percentages are combined to arrive at a percentage mark for the whole qualification.

Grade definition	Percentage threshold
Distinction	90–100%
Merit	80–89%
Pass	70–79%
Unclassified	0–69% Or failure to pass one or more assessment/s

Re-sits

The AAT Professional Diploma In Accounting is not subject to re-sit restrictions.

You should only be entered for an assessment when you are well prepared and you expect to pass the assessment.

AAT qualifications

The material in this book may support the following AAT qualifications:

AAT Professional Diploma in Accounting Level 4 and AAT Professional Diploma in Accounting at SCQF Level 8.

Supplements

From time to time we may need to publish supplementary materials to one of our titles. This can be for a variety of reasons. From a small change in the AAT unit guidance to new legislation coming into effect between editions.

You should check our supplements page regularly for anything that may affect your learning materials. All supplements are available free of charge on our supplements page on our website at:

www.bpp.com/learning-media/about/students

Improving material and removing errors

There is a constant need to update and enhance our study materials in line with both regulatory changes and new insights into the assessments.

From our team of authors BPP appoints a subject expert to update and improve these materials for each new edition.

Their updated draft is subsequently technically checked by another author and from time to time non-technically checked by a proof reader.

We are very keen to remove as many numerical errors and narrative typos as we can but given the volume of detailed information being changed in a short space of time we know that a few errors will sometimes get through our net.

We apologise in advance for any inconvenience that an error might cause. We continue to look for new ways to improve these study materials and would welcome your suggestions. If you have any comments about this book, the BPP author of this edition can be emailed at: learning media@bpp.com.

Question Bank

Chapter 1 – Tax framework

Task 1.1

Listed below are 3 different methods of operating a business.

Put a tick in the relevant column to say whether the business method is incorporated or unincorporated.

	Incorporated ✓	Unincorporated ✓
Sole trader		
Partnership		
Limited company		

Task 1.2

The profits generated by different business methods suffer different taxes.

Show which taxes are suffered by profits generated by each business method by linking the following business methods to the appropriate taxes in the right-hand boxes.

Sole trader	Income tax
Partners	National Insurance Contributions
Company	Capital Gains tax
	Corporation tax

Task 1.3

Listed below are several sources of tax law and practice.

Put a tick in the relevant column to say whether the source has the force of law or not.

	Force of law ✓	No force of law ✓
Statute law		
Act of Parliament		
Statutory Instrument		
HMRC guidance		
Case Law		

Task 1.4

Which of the following actions by a taxpayer would not constitute tax evasion?

	✓
Claiming capital allowances on a fictitious piece of equipment	
Failing to notify HMRC of a profitable trade commenced three years ago	
Obtaining tax-free interest by investing in an ISA	
Deciding not to declare rental income received	

Task 1.5

List TWO ethical duties and responsibilities of an accountant.

Task 1.6

Tax [▼] is the use of loopholes in tax legislation to minimise tax liabilities.

Tax [▼] is the use of all available reliefs in the manner intended to minimise tax liabilities.

Tax [▼] is the deliberate misleading of tax authorities to minimise tax liabilities.

Picklist:

avoidance
evasion
planning

Chapter 2 – Computing trading income

Task 2.1

When deciding whether a trade is being carried on, HM Revenue and Customs is often guided by the badges of trade.

Write a memo to a client who is concerned they may be trading, explaining what is meant by the term badges of trade.

From:	AAT student
To:	A Client
Date:	14 June
Subject:	Badges of trade

This page is for the continuation of your memo. You may not need all of it.

Task 2.2

Decide how each of the following items would be treated in the tax computation of a sole trader. Tick ONE box per line.

	Allow ✓	Disallow and add back ✓	Not taxable so deduct ✓
Gifts of 30 bottles of wine to clients			
Lease costs of a car with emissions of 150g/km			
Costs of £5,000 to repair a roof			
£1,000 cost to register a patent			
Accounting profit on disposal of a van			
£500 donation to a political party			
Depreciation			

Task 2.3

The statement of profit or loss for Mr Jelly for the year ended 31 December shows:

	£		£
Staff wages	12,500	Gross profit from trading account	20,000
Light and heat	162		
Motor car expenses	350		
Postage, stationery and telephone	100		
Repairs and renewals	450		
Irrecoverable debts	238		

	£		£
Miscellaneous expenses	300		
Depreciation charge	600		
Profit for the year	5,300		
	20,000		20,000

The following information is also relevant:

(1)   The staff wages include £260 paid to Mr Jelly.
(2)   One-seventh of the motor expenses relates to private motoring.
(3)   Repairs and renewals comprise:

	£
Painting shop internally	129
Plant repairs	220
Building extension to stockroom	101
	450

(4)   **Irrecoverable debt provisions**

		£			£
			Jan 1	Balances b/f	
Dec 31	Balances c/f			General	200
	General	400		Specific	360
	Specific	398			
			Dec 31	Statement of profit or loss	238
		798			798

(5) **Miscellaneous expenses include:**

	£
Donations – Oxfam	10
Advertising	115
Customer entertaining	90
Christmas gifts – ten bottles of gin and whisky	70
Legal expenses re debt collecting	15
	300

Using the proforma layout provided, compute Mr Jelly's taxable trading profit for the year ended 31 December. Input 0 (zero) if necessary, in order to fill in all unshaded boxes.

	£	£
Profit for the year per accounts		
	Add	Deduct
Staff wages		
Mr Jelly's salary		
Light and heat		
Motor expenses		
Postage, stationery and telephone		
Painting shop internally		
Plant repairs		
Stockroom extension		
Provision		
Donations		
Advertising		
Entertaining		
Gifts		
Legal expenses		
Depreciation charge		
Total net adjustments		
Taxable trading profit		

Task 2.4

Decide how each of the following items would be treated in the tax computation of a sole trader. Tick ONE box per line.

	Allow ✓	Disallow and add back ✓	Not taxable so deduct ✓
Increase in specific provision			
Decrease in general provision			
Depreciation charge			
Cocktail party held for customers			
Political donation			
Employees salary			
Repair to factory roof			

Task 2.5

Bill has trading receipts of £800. Assuming Bill makes any beneficial elections, state below what his taxable trading income will be with the different levels of expenses and whether or not he needs to make an election.

Bill	Taxable trading income	Election required? (Y/N)
Expenses of £200		
Expenses of £900		

Belinda has trading receipts of £1,500. Assuming Belinda makes any beneficial elections, state below what her taxable trading income will be with the different levels of expenses and whether or not she needs to make an election.

Belinda	Taxable trading income	Election required? (Y/N)
Expenses of £1,200		
Expenses of £300		

Task 2.6

Graham has carried on business for many years making up accounts to 31 March each year.

The following information is relevant to his period of account to 31 March 2021:

	£
Revenue	150,000
Cost of goods bought	25,000
Heating	1,200
Insurance	560
Office costs	1,700
Bank charges	150
Accountancy and legal costs (£500 disallowable as relates to capital)	1,650
Goods taken for own use (market value)	750
New car (CO_2 emissions 170 g/km)	19,000

Using this information, complete the self-employment page below.

Business expenses

Please read the 'Self-employment (full) notes' before filling in this section.

Total expenses	Disallowable expenses
If your annual turnover was below £85,000, you may just put your total expenses in box 31	Use this column if the figures in boxes 17 to 30 include disallowable amounts

17 Cost of goods bought for resale or goods used

£ [   ] · 0 0

32 £ [   ] · 0 0

18 Construction industry – payments to subcontractors

£ [   ] · 0 0

33 £ [   ] · 0 0

19 Wages, salaries and other staff costs

£ [   ] · 0 0

34 £ [   ] · 0 0

20 Car, van and travel expenses

£ [   ] · 0 0

35 £ [   ] · 0 0

21 Rent, rates, power and insurance costs

£ [   ] · 0 0

36 £ [   ] · 0 0

22 Repairs and maintenance of property and equipment

£ [   ] · 0 0

37 £ [   ] · 0 0

23 Phone, fax, stationery and other office costs

£ [   ] · 0 0

38 £ [   ] · 0 0

24 Advertising and business entertainment costs

£ [   ] · 0 0

39 £ [   ] · 0 0

25 Interest on bank and other loans

£ [   ] · 0 0

40 £ [   ] · 0 0

26 Bank, credit card and other financial charges

£ [   ] · 0 0

41 £ [   ] · 0 0

27 Irrecoverable debts written off

£ [   ] · 0 0

42 £ [   ] · 0 0

28 Accountancy, legal and other professional fees

£ [   ] · 0 0

43 £ [   ] · 0 0

29 Depreciation and loss or profit on sale of assets

£ [   ] · 0 0

44 £ [   ] · 0 0

30 Other business expenses

£ [   ] · 0 0

45 £ [   ] · 0 0

31 Total expenses (total of boxes 17 to 30)

£ [   ] · 0 0

46 Total disallowable expenses (total of boxes 32 to 45)

£ [   ] · 0 0

SA103F 2021   Page SEF 2

(Adapted from HMRC, 2020)

Chapter 3 – Capital allowances

Task 3.1

For the following items of expenditure, tick if they are revenue or capital, and if they are eligible for capital allowances:

	Revenue ✓	Capital ✓	Capital allowances
Purchase of machinery			
Rent paid for premises			
Insurance of premises			
Repairs to roof of factory			
New extension to shop			
Installation of new picture window			
Purchase of new car for owner			
Legal fees relating to purchase of new factory			
Payment of staff wages			
Accountancy costs			
Redecoration of shop			

Task 3.2

Bodie, a sole trader, makes up a set of accounts for the 18 months ending 30 April 2020. The value of the main pool as at 1 November 2018 was £38,500.

His expenditure, all qualifying for capital allowances, has been as follows:

Date		£
14 January 2019	Factory machinery	1,500,000
30 March 2019	Mercedes car – CO_2 emissions 105g/km	18,000
31 March 2019	Car – CO_2 emissions 100g/km	8,000
2 June 2019	Office equipment	31,000

The Mercedes was for the proprietor's own use (20% private), while the other car was for an employee.

Machinery which had been acquired for £7,000 was sold for £3,000 on 31 December 2019 .

Using the proforma layout provided, calculate capital allowances for the period ending 30 April 2020.

Task 3.3

Wolfgang commences to trade on 1 April 2020. During his first year, he incurs the following expenditure:

		£
6 May 2020	Machinery	850,000
6 July 2020	Car with CO_2 emissions of 40g/km	8,000
31 August 2020	Car with CO_2 emissions of 105g/km	10,500

Using the proforma layout provided, compute the capital allowances available to Wolfgang for the year ended 31 March 2021.

Task 3.4

Rachel is a sole trader who changed her accounting date from 31 March to 30 September with a short accounting period ending 30 September 2020.

On 1 April 2020, the brought forward balances on her plant and machinery were as follows:

	£
Main pool	120,000
Car – private use 30% by Rachel	21,000
Special rate pool	17,500

She sold the car she used privately for £16,000 on 10 August 2020 and bought another car (CO_2 emissions 170g/km) on the same day for £25,000, which also had 30% private use by her.

Using the proforma layout provided, calculate the capital allowances available in the six months to 30 September 2020.

Task 3.5

At the end of the period of account to 28 February 2019 the value of the main pool in Green Ltd's tax computations was £106,000.

On 1 January 2020 a car costing £14,000 was acquired. The CO_2 emissions of the car were 170 g/km, and was used privately 30% of the time by the Finance Director.

There were no other purchases or sales during the year. The company had always prepared accounts to the end of February

Using the proforma layout provided, calculate the capital allowances available in the year ended 29 February 2020.

Task 3.6

Davies Ltd prepares accounts annually to 31 March.

During the accounting period ended 31 March 2021, Davies Ltd purchased and disposed of the following items of plant and machinery.

		£
Purchases		
10 May 2020	A machine	1,060,000
16 August 2020	A car	
	(CO_2 emissions 119g/km)	22,000
12 December 2020	Computer with a useful life of six years. A short life asset election will be made.	12,000
Disposals		
10 June 2020	A laser cutting machine, originally purchased in June 2019 for £17,500 was sold. The tax written down value of this asset on 1 April 2020 was £14,000. An election has been made to treat this machine as a short life asset.	12,000

The tax written down value of the main pool on 1 April 2020 was £180,000.

Davies Ltd can claim capital allowances for the year ended 31 March 2021 of £ ☐ .

Workings

Task 3.7

XYZ plc had the following transactions in plant and machinery for the nine-month period ended 31 March 2021:

		£
Purchases		
10 July 2020	A machine	775,000
16 August 2020	A BMW with CO_2 emissions of 108g/km used privately by an employee 20% of his time	19,000
1 January 2021	An Audi with CO_2 emissions of 120g/km	25,000
Disposals		
10 January 2021	A machine, which had originally cost £8,500, was sold for £6,600.	6,600

The tax written down value of the main pool on 1 July 2020 was £230,000.

XYZ plc can claim capital allowances for the period ended 31 March 2021 of £ ☐ .

Workings

Chapter 4 – Computing corporation tax

Task 4.1

Geronimo Ltd's summarised statement of profit or loss for the year ended 31 March 2021 is as follows:

	£	£
Gross profit		925,940
Operating expenses		
Depreciation charge	83,420	
Gifts (note 1)	2,850	
Professional fees (note 2)	14,900	
Repairs and renewals (note 3)	42,310	
Other expenses (all allowable)	165,980	
		(309,460)
Operating profit		616,480
Income from investments		
Debenture interest (note 4)	24,700	
Bank interest (note 4)	4,800	
Dividends (note 5)	56,000	
		85,500
		701,980
Interest payable on loans for trading purposes		(45,000)
Profit for the year before taxation		656,980

Note.

1   Gifts

Gifts are as follows:

	£
Qualifying charitable donation	1,900
Donation to local charity (Geronimo Ltd received free advertising in the charity's magazine)	50
Gifts to customers (food hampers costing £30 each)	900
	2,850

Note.

2   Professional fees

Professional fees are as follows:

	£
Accountancy and audit fee	4,100
Legal fees in connection with the renewal of a 20-year property lease	2,400
Legal fees in connection with the issue of a debenture loan for trade purposes	8,400
	14,900

Note.

3   Repairs and renewals

The figure of £42,310 for repairs includes £6,200 for replacing part of a wall that was knocked down by a lorry, and £12,200 for initial repairs to an office building that was acquired during the year ended 31 March 2020. The office building was not usable until the repairs were carried out, and this fact was represented by a reduced purchase price.

Note.

4   Bank interest

The bank interest and the debenture interest were both received on non-trade investments.

Note.

5   Dividends received

The dividends were received from other companies. The figure of £56,000 is the actual amount received.

Note.

6   Capital allowances

Capital allowances for the year have been calculated as £13,200.

Using the proforma layout provided, calculate Geronimo Ltd's taxable trading profit for the year ended 31 March 2021. Use brackets for deductions and insert 0 (zero) if necessary, in order to fill in all unshaded boxes.

	£	£
Profit per accounts		656,980
	Add	Deduct
Depreciation charge		
Qualifying charitable donation		
Donation to local charity		
Gifts to customers		
Accountancy and audit fee		
Legal fees – renewal of 20 year lease		
Legal fees – issue of debenture		
Repairs – knocked down wall		
Initial repairs to office		
Other expenses		
Debenture interest		
Bank interest		

	£	£
Dividends		
Capital allowances		
Interest payable on trading loans		
Net adjustments		
Taxable trading profit		

Task 4.2

Decide how each of the following items would be treated in the tax computation of a company with respect to its trading profits. Tick ONE box per line.

	Allow ✓	Disallow and add back ✓	Not taxable as trading income so deduct ✓
Dividends received from an unconnected company			
Profit on sale of shares			
Running costs of car with 20% private use by an employee			
Parking fine of director			
Capital allowances			
Director's salary			
Bank interest received			

Task 4.3

Righteous plc used to make its accounts up to 31 December. However, the directors decided to change the accounting date to 31 May and make up accounts for a 17-month period to 31 May 2021. The following information relates to the period of account from 1 January 2020 to 31 May 2021:

	£
Adjusted trading profit	500,000
Property business income	15,300
Capital gain on property sold on:	
1 May 2021	3,000
Qualifying charitable donations paid on:	
28 February 2020	15,000
31 August 2020	15,000
28 February 2021	40,000

No capital allowances are claimed.

Using the proforma layout provided, compute taxable total profits for the accounting periods based on the above accounts. Use brackets for deductions and insert 0 (zero) if necessary, in order to fill in all unshaded boxes.

	Year to 31 December 2020 £	Five months to 31 May 2021 £
Trading profits		
Property business income		
Chargeable gain		
Total profits		
Qualifying charitable donations paid		
Taxable total profits		

Task 4.4

When a company has a period of account which exceeds 12 months, how are the following apportioned:

	Time apportioned ✓	Period in which arises ✓	Separate computation ✓
Capital allowances			
Trading income			
Property income			
Interest income			
Chargeable gain			

Task 4.5

Rosemary Ltd has the following results for the ten-month period ended 31 March 2021:

	£
Taxable trading profits	600,000
Property business income	300,000
Dividends received	162,000

The corporation tax payable by Rosemary Ltd for period ended 31 March 2021 is:

£	

Chapter 5 – Taxing unincorporated businesses

Task 5.1

Rachel commenced in business as a fashion designer on 1 January 2019, and made up her first accounts to 30 April 2020. Her profit for the period, adjusted for taxation, was £33,000.

Her first tax year is:

Her taxable profits in her first tax year of trading are:

£ | |

Her taxable profits in her second tax year of trading are:

£ | |

Her taxable profits in her third tax year of trading are:

£ | |

Overlap profits are:

£ | |

Task 5.2

Mr Phone commenced trading on 1 July 2018 making up accounts to 31 May each year.

Profits are:

	£
1 July 2018 to 31 May 2019	22,000
Year ended 31 May 2020	18,000
Year ended 31 May 2021	30,000

Mr Phone's basis period for 2018/19 runs from: (insert the date as xx/xx/xxxx)

to:

[ ]

Mr Phone's basis period for 2019/20 runs from: (insert the date as xx/xx/xxxx)

[ ]

to:

[ ]

His taxable profits in his second tax year of trading are:

£ [ ]

Overlap profits are:

£ [ ]

Task 5.3

Mr Mug ceased trading on 31 December 2020. His overlap profits brought forward amount to £9,000. His profits for the last few periods of account were:

	£
Year ended 30 April 2018	36,000
Year ended 30 April 2019	48,000
Year ended 30 April 2020	16,000
Eight months ended 31 December 2020	4,000

Mr Mug's final tax year is: (insert as xxxx/xx)

[ ]

Mr Mug's penultimate tax year is: (insert as xxxx/xx)

[ ]

His taxable profits in his final tax year of trading are:

£ [ ]

Task 5.4

Jackie Smith started her picture framing business on 1 May 2016. Due to falling profits she ceased to trade on 29 February 2021.

Her profits for the whole period of trading were as follows.

	£
1 May 2016 – 31 July 2017	18,000
1 August 2017 – 31 July 2018	11,700
1 August 2018 – 31 July 2019	8,640
1 August 2019 – 31 July 2020	4,800
1 August 2020 – 29 February 2021	5,100

Jackie's first tax year is: (insert as xxxx/xx)

Her taxable profits in her first tax year of trading are:

£

Jackie's second tax year is: (insert as xxxx/xx)

Her taxable profits in her second tax year of trading are:

£

Jackie's final tax year is: (insert as xxxx/xx)

Her taxable profits in her final tax year of trading are:

£

Over the life of her business Jackie is assessed on total profits of:

£

Task 5.5

Matilda changed her accounting date from 31 March to 31 December. Her accounting periods were as follows:

- Year ended 31 March 2019
- Period ending 31 December 2019
- Year ended 31 December 2020

The year of change for Matilda's business is:

[   ]

Her basis period for the tax year 2018/19 is:

[   ]

Her basis period for the tax year 2019/20 is:

[   ]

Her basis period for the tax year 2020/21 is:

[   ]

Chapter 6 – Partnerships

Task 6.1

Fimbo and Florrie commenced in partnership on 1 January 2019. They produce accounts to 31 December each year and their profits have been as follows:

	Taxable profit £
Year ended 31 December 2019	10,000
Year ended 31 December 2020	20,000
Year ended 31 December 2021	25,000

Until 31 December 2020 Fimbo took 60% of the profits after receiving a £5,000 salary. Florrie took the remaining 40% of profits.

On 1 January 2021, Fimbo and Florrie invite Pom to join the partnership. It is agreed that Fimbo's salary will increase to £6,500 and the profits will then be split equally between the three partners.

Using the proforma layout provided, show the division of profit for the three periods of account. Fill in all unshaded boxes. Insert a 0 (zero) if necessary.

	Total £	Fimbo £	Florrie £	Pom £
12 months to 31 December 2019				
Salary				
Share of profits				
Total for year				
12 months to 31 December 2020				
Salary				
Share of profits				
Total for year				
12 months to 31 December 2021				
Salary				
Share of profits				
Total for year				

Task 6.2

John, Paul and George began to trade as partners on 1 January 2018. The profits of the partnership are shared in the ratio 4:3:3. The accounts for recent periods have shown the following results:

	£
Period to 31 July 2018	24,300
Year to 31 July 2019	16,200
Year to 31 July 2020	14,900

(a) **Using the proforma layout provided, show the allocation of trading profits for all three periods of account. Fill in all unshaded boxes. Insert a 0 (zero) if necessary.**

	Total £	John £	Paul £	George £
Period ended 31 July 2018				
Division of profits				
Year ended 31 July 2019				
Division of profits				
Year ended 31 July 2020				
Division of profits				

(b) **Using the proforma layout provided, calculate the taxable trading profits of John, Paul and George for all tax years. Fill in all boxes.**

	John £	Paul £	George £
2017/18			
2018/19			
2019/20			
2020/21			

Task 6.3

Strange and his partners Pavin and Lehman had traded for many years. Strange had contributed £20,000 to the business and Pavin £10,000.

Profits were shared in the ratio of 3:2:1 after providing Strange and Pavin with salaries of £15,000 and £5,000 and interest on capital of 5%.

On 1 August 2020 the profit sharing arrangements were changed to 2:2:1 after providing only Strange with a salary of £20,000, and no further interest on capital for any of the partners.

The partnership profit for the year to 31 December 2020 was £48,000.

Using the proforma layout provided, show the allocation of profit for the year to 31 December 2020. Fill in all unshaded boxes. Insert a 0 (zero) if necessary.

Year ended 31 December 2020	Total £	Strange £	Pavin £	Lehman £
To 31 July 2020				
Salaries				
Interest on capital				
Division of profits				
To 31 December 2020				
Salary				
Division of profits				
Total for year ended 31 December 2020				

Task 6.4

Bob, Annie and John started their partnership on 1 June 2011 and make accounts up to 31 May each year. The accounts have always shown taxable profits.

For the period up to 31 January 2020 each partner received a salary of £15,000 per annum and the remaining profits were shared 50% to Bob and 25% each to Annie and John. There was no interest on capital.

Bob left the partnership on 1 February 2020. The profit sharing ratio, after the same salaries, changed to 50% each to Annie and John.

Profits for the year ending 31 May 2020 were £90,000.

Using the proforma layout provided, calculate each partner's share of the profits for the year to 31 May 2020. Fill in all unshaded boxes. Insert a 0 (zero) if necessary.

Year ended 31 May 2020	Total £	Bob £	Annie £	John £
To 31 January 2020				
Salaries				
Division of profits				
To 31 May 2020				
Salaries				
Division of profits				
Total for year ended 31 May 2020				

Task 6.5

This style of task is human marked in the live assessment.

Anne Curtis and Bettina Stone have been trading in partnership selling designer dresses for many years, making up accounts to 31 December each year. They share profits equally.

The following information relates to the year to 31 December 2020:

	£
Revenue	125,000
Cost of goods bought	75,000
Rental of shop	12,000
General administration	1,700
Accountancy	650
Goods taken for own use (market value)	1,550
New sewing machine for alterations	1,200
The partnership received interest in the year to 5 April 2021 of:	
Bank interest received	8,000

Using this information, complete page 6 of the Partnership Tax return which follows for Anne Curtis.

(Adapted from HMRC, 2020)

Chapter 7 – National insurance

Task 7.1

Abraham has trading profits of £12,830 for the year ended 31 December 2020.

The Class 2 NIC liability for 2020/21 is:

£ [   ] . [   ]

The Class 4 NIC liability for 2020/21 is:

£ [   ] . [   ]

The total NIC liability for 2020/21 is:

£ [   ] . [   ]

Task 7.2

John has profits of £58,000 for the year ended 31 March 2021.

The Class 2 NIC liability for 2020/21 is:

£ [   ] . [   ]

The Class 4 NIC liability for 2020/21 is:

£ [   ] . [   ]

The total NIC liability for 2020/21 is:

£ [   ] . [   ]

Task 7.3

Raj has trading profits of £3,500 for 2020/21.

The Class 2 NIC liability for 2020/21 is:

£ [   ] . [   ]

The Class 4 NIC liability for 2020/21 is:

£ [   ] . [   ]

The total NIC liability for 2020/21 is:

£ [   ] . [   ]

Task 7.4

Zoë is a self employed author who starts in business on 6 April 2020. In the year to 5 April 2021 she had taxable trading profits of £80,000.

The Class 2 NIC liability for 2020/21 is:

£ [   ] . [   ]

The Class 4 NIC liability for 2020/21 is:

£ [   ] . [   ]

The total NIC liability for 2020/21 is:

£ [   ] . [   ]

Task 7.5

Wendy and Jayne have been in partnership as interior designers for many years, trading as Dramatic Decors.

On 1 January 2021, Wendy and Jayne admitted Paula to the partnership. From that date, partnership profits were shared 40% to each of Wendy and Jayne and 20% to Paula. The partnership continued to make up its accounts to 31 December and the trading profit for the year to 31 December 2021 was £280,000.

Paula had not worked for many years prior to becoming a partner in Dramatic Decors.

(a)   The share of profits taxable on Paula for 2020/21 is:

£ [   ]

and for 2021/22 is:

£ [   ]

and the overlap profits to carry forward are:

£ [   ]

(b)   The Class 4 NIC payable by Paula for 2020/21 are:

£ [   ] . [   ]

Chapter 8 – Losses

Task 8.1

Pipchin has traded for many years, making up accounts to 30 September each year. His recent results have been:

Year ended	£
30 September 2018	12,000
30 September 2019	(45,000)
30 September 2020	8,000
30 September 2021	14,000

He has received property income as follows:

	£
2018/19	10,400
2019/20	11,000
2020/21	11,000
2021/22	11,000

Using the proforma layout provided, compute Pipchin's net income for 2018/19 to 2021/22, assuming maximum claims for loss relief are made as early as possible. If an answer is zero, insert 0, and show the offset of losses within brackets. Fill in all boxes.

	2018/19 £	2019/20 £	2020/21 £	2021/22 £
Trading profits				
Trading loss offset against future year				
Property income				
Trading loss offset against current year				
Trading loss offset against previous year				
Net income				

Task 8.2

Identify whether the following statement is true or false.

An individual can restrict a claim to set a trading loss against total income in order to have enough net income to use his personal allowance.

	✓
True	
False	

Task 8.3

Identify whether the following statement is true or false.

An individual must make a trading loss claim against total income in the tax year of the loss before making a claim to set the loss against total income in the preceding year.

	✓
True	
False	

Task 8.4

Identify whether the following statement is true or false.

An individual can only carry a trading loss forward against trading income of the same trade.

	✓
True	
False	

Task 8.5

Pennington Ltd produced the following results:

| | Year ended 31 March | | |
	2019 £	2020 £	2021 £
Trading profit/(loss)	62,000	20,000	(83,000)
NTLR income	1,200	600	1,200
Qualifying charitable donation	100	50	100

(a) **Using the proforma layout provided, compute Pennington Ltd's taxable total profits for the above accounting periods, assuming the loss relief is claimed as soon as possible. Fill in all boxes. Use brackets for loss relief and add a 0 (zero) where necessary.**

| | Year ended 31 March | | |
	2019 £	2020 £	2021 £
Trading profits			
NTLR income			
Total profits			
Current period loss relief			
Carry back loss relief			
Total profits after loss relief			
Qualifying charitable donation			
Taxable total profits			

(b) **The trading loss available to carry forward at 31 March 2021 is:**

£ [   ]

Task 8.6

Ferraro Ltd has the following results.

	Year ended 30.6.18 £	9 months to 31.3.19 £	Year ended 31.3.20 £	Year ended 31.3.21 £
Trading profit (loss)	6,200	4,320	(100,000)	53,000
Bank deposit interest accrued	80	240	260	200
Rents receivable	1,420	1,440	1,600	1,500
Chargeable gain	–	12,680	–	–
Allowable capital loss	(5,000)	–	(9,423)	
Qualifying charitable donation	1,000	1,000	1,500	–

(a) **Using the proforma layout provided, compute all taxable total profits, claiming loss reliefs as early as possible. Fill in all boxes. Use brackets for loss relief and add a 0 (zero) where necessary.**

	Year ended 30.6.18 £	9 months to 31.3.19 £	Year ended 31.3.20 £	Year ended 31.3.21 £
Trading profits				
NTLR income				
Property income				
Chargeable gains				
Total profits				

	Year ended 30.6.18 £	9 months to 31.3.19 £	Year ended 31.3.20 £	Year ended 31.3.21 £
Current period loss relief				
Carry back loss relief				
Carry forward loss relief				
Total profits after loss relief				
Qualifying charitable donation				
Taxable total profits				

(b) **The trading loss available to carry forward at 31 March 2021 is:**

£ [   ]

(c) **The capital loss available to carry forward at 31 March 2021 is:**

£ [   ]

Task 8.7

Identify whether the following statement is true or false.

A company must offset its trading loss against total profits in the loss-making period before carrying the loss back.

	✓
True	
False	

Task 8.8

Identify whether the following statement is true or false.

If a company carries a trading loss forward, the company can elect how much of the loss can be set against total profits in the following accounting period.

	✓
True	
False	

∎∙∙∙

Task 8.9

Identify whether the following statement is true or false.

A company can set-off a capital loss against trading profits.

	✓
True	
False	

∎∙∙∙

Chapter 9 – Self assessment for individuals

Task 9.1

Identify by which date an individual should normally submit their 2020/21 self-assessment tax return if it is to be filed online. Tick ONE box.

	✓
31 January 2022	
5 April 2022	
31 October 2021	
31 December 2021	

Task 9.2

Gordon had income tax payable of £14,500 in 2019/20. His income tax payable for 2020/21 was £20,500.

How will Gordon settle his income tax payable for 2020/21? Tick ONE box.

	✓
The full amount of £20,500 will be paid on 31 January 2022.	
Payments on account based on the estimated 2020/21 liability will be made on 31 January and 31 July 2021, with the balance payable on 31 January 2022.	
Payments on account of £10,250 will be made on 31 January and 31 July 2021 with nothing due on 31 January 2022.	
Payments on account of £7,250 will be made on 31 January and 31 July 2021, with the balance of £6,000 being paid on 31 January 2022.	

Task 9.3

The minimum penalty as a percentage of Potential Lost Revenue for a deliberate and concealed error on a tax return where there is a prompted disclosure is:

	✓
100%	
50%	
35%	
15%	

....

Task 9.4

Identify whether the following statement is true or false.

If an individual files her 2020/21 return online on 13 April 2022, the penalty for late filing is £100.

	✓
True	
False	

....

Task 9.5

Identify whether the following statement is true or false.

The penalty for failure to keep records is £3,000 per tax year or accounting period.

	✓
True	
False	

....

Task 9.6

Identify whether the following statement is true or false.

An individual is required to make a payment on account on 31 July 2021 for 2020/21. The payment is actually made on 10 November 2021.

The penalty payable is 5%.

	✓
True	
False	

....

Chapter 10 – Self assessment for companies

Task 10.1

Boscobel plc has been a large company for corporation tax purposes for many years. For the year ending 31 March 2021, it had a corporation tax liability of £500,000.

Fill in the table below showing how it will pay its corporation tax liability.

Instalment	Due date (xx/xx/xxxx)	Amount due £
1		
2		
3		
4		

Task 10.2

Tick whether the following statements are true or false.

	True ✓	False ✓
A company with a period of account ending on 31 March 2021 must keep its records until 31 March 2023.		
The due date for payment of CGT for 2020/21 is 31 January 2022.		
An individual who becomes chargeable to income tax in 2020/21 must notify HMRC by 31 October 2021.		
A large company will not have to pay corporation tax by instalments if it has profits not exceeding £10m and was not large in the previous accounting period.		
A company which is not large (for corporation tax purposes) must pay its corporation tax by nine months and one day after the end of its accounting period.		

BPP
LEARNING MEDIA

Task 10.3

A company receives a notice to file its return for the year ended 31 December 2020 on 28 November 2021.

The corporation tax return must be filed by:

\
```



```

A company receives a notice to file its return for the year ended 30 June 2020 on 15 July 2020.

The corporation tax return must be filed by:

```



```

Task 10.4

A company must keep its accounting records for ☐ **years.**

Failure to do so may incur a penalty of £ ☐ .

Task 10.5

Fred works as an IT Consultant and derives nearly all of his income from one main client, Bishopston Ltd. Fred uses his Personal Service Company, Fred Services Ltd to invoice Bishopston Ltd, and then extracts most of the income from his company via dividends. Fred works from home, using a Bishopston Ltd laptop and is permitted under the agreement with Bishopston Ltd to get someone else to perform the work when he is on holiday or unwell.

Explain which aspects of this scenario suggest that the IR35 rules may or may not apply.

Explain what difference it would make to how Fred is taxed if the IR35 rules are imposed.

Task 10.6

A small company spends £50,000 on Research and Development staff and consumables in the year ended 30 June 2020.

The amount which is deductible as a trading expense is

£ [   ].

If this resulted in a loss, the loss could be surrendered in exchange for a tax credit at the rate of [   ] %

Chapter 11 – Chargeable gains – the basics

Task 11.1

Complete the following sentence by filling in the gaps:

For the gain on the disposal of a capital asset to be a chargeable gain there must be a chargeable ⬚ **of a chargeable** ⬚ **by a chargeable** ⬚.

Task 11.2

Identify whether the following assets are chargeable assets or exempt assets for CGT:

Item	Chargeable ✓	Exempt ✓
Wasting chattel with useful life of 25 years		
Disposal of half the holding of a plot of land		
Car used for business purposes		

Task 11.3

Romana purchased a freehold holiday cottage for £40,000. She then spent £5,000 building a new conservatory on the cottage. She sold the cottage for £90,600 on 15 March 2021. Romana had not made any other disposals during 2020/21.

What is her taxable gain for 2020/21?

	✓
£33,300	
£38,300	
£45,600	
£50,600	

Task 11.4

In August 2020 George made chargeable gains of £20,000 and allowable losses of £3,560. He made no other disposals during 2020/21 and he is a higher rate taxpayer.

(a)   George's capital gains tax liability for 2020/21 is:

£ [   ]

(b)   George's capital gains tax liability is payable by:

[   ]

Task 11.5

Jack sells an asset in December 2020 and makes a chargeable gain of £15,000. Jack is an additional rate taxpayer.

At what rate would Jack pay capital gains tax on this gain?

[   ] %

Task 11.6

In November 2020, Graham made chargeable gains of £15,000 and allowable losses of £5,200. He made no other disposals during 2020/21.

The amount of the loss Graham will use in 2020/21 is:

£ [   ]

Task 11.7

Gayle made chargeable gains of £5,000 in August 2020 and £18,100 in November 2020. In July 2020 she made allowable losses of £2,000. She has unused basic rate band of £5,000 in 2020/21.

Gayle's capital gains tax liability for 2020/21 is:

£ [   ]

Task 11.8

Gerry made chargeable gains of £27,100 in December 2020. She made no other disposals in the year. Her taxable income (ie after deducting the personal allowance) for 2020/21 was £26,005. Note the limit for the basic rate band for 2020/21 is £37,500.

Gerry's capital gains tax liability for 2020/21 is:

£ [   ]

....

Task 11.9

Kevin made gains of £20,900 and losses of £6,600 in 2020/21. He has losses brought forward of £5,000.

The losses to carry forward to 2021/22 are:

£ [   ]

....

Task 11.10

Elias has the following gains and losses arising from disposals of chargeable assets:

Tax year	2018/19 £	2019/20 £	2020/21 £
Gains	2,000	4,000	14,900
Losses	(14,000)	(2,000)	(2,000)

The maximum allowable loss carried forward to 2021/22 will be:

£ [   ]

....

Task 11.11

On 14 April 2020, Fire Ltd sold a factory for £230,000. This had originally been purchased in April 2003 for £160,000.

Assumed Indexation factor

April 2003 – December 2017   0.535

Using the proforma layout provided calculate the chargeable gain arising on the disposal of the factory. Fill in all boxes. Add a 0 (zero) if necessary.

	£
Proceeds	
Less cost	
Unindexed gain	
Less indexation allowance	
Chargeable gain/allowable loss	

Task 11.12

On 18 July 2020, Earth plc sold a warehouse for £180,000. This had been purchased in May 2006 for £100,000. Earth plc had spent £25,000 on an extension to the warehouse in August 2008.

Assumed Indexation factors

May 2006 – December 2017	0.407
May 2006 – August 2008	0.080
August 2008 – December 2017	0.280

Using the proforma layout provided calculate the chargeable gain arising on the disposal of the warehouse. Fill in all boxes. Add a 0 (zero) if necessary.

	£
Proceeds	
Less: cost	
enhancement expenditure	
Unindexed gain	
Less: indexation allowance on cost	
indexation allowance on enhancement	
Chargeable gain	

Task 11.13

Identify whether the following statement is true or false.

A company is entitled to an annual exempt amount.

	✓
True	
False	

Chapter 12 – Further aspects of chargeable gains

Task 12.1

Harry bought a three-acre plot of land for £150,000. He sold two acres of the land at auction for £240,000. His disposal costs were £3,000. The market value of the one remaining acre at the date of sale was £60,000.

(a) **The cost of the land sold is:**

£	

(b) **The gain on sale is:**

£	

Task 12.2

Leonora purchased a picture for £5,500 and sold it in September for £7,500, incurring £300 expenses of sale.

Her chargeable gain on sale is:

	✓
£2,300	
£2,000	
£2,500	
£1,700	

Task 12.3

Mark purchased an antique vase for £9,000. He sold the vase in August at auction for £4,500 net of auctioneer's fees of 10%.

Mark's allowable loss is:

£	

Task 12.4

Identify whether the following statement is true or false.

Chloe bought a necklace for £4,000. She sold it in September for £5,500.

Chloe has a chargeable gain on sale of £1,500.

	✓
True	
False	

Task 12.5

In August 2020, John gave his daughter an asset worth £10,000. He had acquired the asset for £25,000.

In March 2021, John gave his brother an asset worth £60,000. John had acquired the asset for £15,000.

John's chargeable gains (before the annual exempt amount) for 2020/21 are:

	✓
£45,000	
£30,000	
£32,700	
£17,700	

Task 12.6

Identify whether the following statement is true or false.

A disposal to a connected person is deemed to be at market value.

	✓
True	
False	

Task 12.7

On 14 November 2020, Wind plc sold two offices for £140,000. These had been part of a large office block. The whole block had cost £250,000 in August 2003 and in November 2020 the remaining offices had a market value of £320,000.

Assumed indexation factor:

August 2003 – December 2017   0.531

(a)   The cost of the two offices disposed of is:

£ [   ]

(b)   The chargeable gain arising on the disposal is:

£ [   ]

Task 12.8

LM plc bought a painting in October 2008 for £4,500. It sold the painting at auction in September 2020 and received £7,500 after deducting the auctioneers' commission of £500. Assume the indexation factor between October 2008 and December 2017 is 0.277.

Complete the following computation.

	£
Proceeds	
Disposal costs	
Cost of acquisition	
Indexation allowance	
Gain	
Gain using chattel marginal relief	
Chargeable gain	

Chapter 13 – Share disposals

Task 13.1

Jake sold 5,000 ordinary shares for £20,000 in JKL plc on 10 August 2020. He bought 6,000 shares in JKL plc for £9,000 on 15 July 2016 and another 1,000 shares for £4,200 on 16 August 2020.

His net gain on sale is:

£	

··

Task 13.2

Susan's dealings in K plc were as follows:

	No. of shares	Cost/(proceeds) £
10 February 2001	12,000	18,000
20 September 2008	Bonus issue of 1 for 4	Nil
15 March 2021	(2,000)	(8,000)

Using the proforma layout provided, calculate the gain on sale. Fill in all unshaded boxes. Use a 0 (zero) if necessary.

Share pool

	No. of shares	Cost £
10 February 2001		
20 September 2008 Bonus 1:4		
Total before disposal		
15 March 2021 Disposal		
c/f		

Gain on sale

	£
Proceeds	
Less cost	
Gain	

....

Task 13.3

This style of task is human marked in the live assessment.

Geoff sold 10,000 of his shares in AC plc on 4 November 2020 for £60,000. The shares had been acquired as follows:

	No. of shares	Cost £
9 December 2001	12,000	4,400
12 October 2005 (rights issue 1:3 at £5)		
10 November 2020	2,000	11,500

Compute the gain or loss made on these shares. Clearly show the balance of shares and their value to carry forward.

....

Task 13.4

Standring Ltd owned 20,000 shares in Smart plc acquired as follows:

5,000 shares acquired September 2001 for £10,000.
1 for 5 rights acquired October 2004 at £5 per share.
14,000 shares acquired August 2006 for £84,000.
Standring Ltd sold 18,000 shares in January 2021 for £155,000.

Indexation factors

September 2001 – October 2004	0.080
October 2004 – August 2006	0.056
August 2006 – December 2017	0.396

Using the proforma layout provided, calculate the chargeable gain arising on the sale in January 2021.

FA 1985 pool

	No. of shares	Original cost £	Indexed cost £

	No. of shares	Original cost £	Indexed cost £

Gain

	£

Task 13.5

Box plc sold 11,000 shares in Crate Ltd for £78,200 on 25 May 2020. These shares had been acquired as follows.

26 May 1995	Purchased	4,000 shares for	£24,000
30 June 1996	1 for 2 bonus issue		
24 October 2003	Purchased	5,000 shares for	£27,500

Indexation factors

May 1995 – October 2003	0.221
May 1995 – June 1996	0.023
June 1996 – October 2003	0.193
October 2003 – December 2017	0.523

Using the proforma layout provided, calculate the gain on disposal.

FA 1985 pool

	No. of shares	Original cost £	Indexed cost £

Gain

	£

Task 13.6

Identify whether the following statement is true or false.

Indexation allowance on rights issue shares runs from the date of the rights issue even though the rights issue shares are treated as having been acquired at the time of the original acquisition to which they relate.

	✓
True	
False	

Task 14.1

Ronald started in business as a sole trader in August 2007. He acquired a freehold shop for £80,000 and a warehouse for £150,000.

He sold his business as a going concern to Lesley in December 2020 and received £50,000 for goodwill, £90,000 for the shop and £130,000 for the warehouse. Ronald made no other chargeable gains in 2020/21 and he is a higher rate taxpayer.

Using the proforma layout provided, compute the CGT payable by Ronald for 2020/21. Fill in all unshaded boxes. Use a 0 (zero) if necessary.

	£	£
Proceeds of goodwill		
Less cost		
Gain/(loss) on goodwill		
Proceeds of shop		
Less cost		
Gain/(loss) on shop		
Proceeds of warehouse		
Less cost		
Gain/(loss) on warehouse		
Net gains eligible for business asset disposal relief		
Less annual exempt amount		
Taxable gains		
CGT payable		

Task 14.2

Identify whether the following statement is true or false.

The lifetime limit of gains eligible for business asset disposal relief is £1,000,000.

	✓
True	
False	

....

Task 14.3

Simon acquired 10,000 Blue Ltd shares worth £65,000 in September 1992 as a gift from his father. His father had originally acquired them as an investment in 1987 and gift relief was claimed on the gain of £15,000. Simon sold the Blue Ltd shares for £200,000 on 30 November 2020. He has no other assets for CGT purposes and made no other disposals in 2020/21.

The taxable gain arising on the sale of the Blue Ltd shares is:

£	

....

Task 14.4

Fran gave a factory worth £500,000 to her friend Anna on 1 June 2020 and a claim for gift relief was made. Fran had bought the factory on 1 January 1997 for £75,000. On 1 July 2021 Anna sold the factory for £520,000.

(a) **Fran's chargeable gain on her disposal is:**

£	

(b) **Anna's chargeable gain on her disposal is:**

£	

....

Task 14.5

On 6 April 1989 Edward acquired for £60,000 a small workshop where he carried on his trade as a furniture maker. On 6 August 2020 he sold the workshop for £125,000 having moved on 10 April 2020 to smaller premises which cost £123,500.

(a) **Edward's gain on the disposal before rollover relief is:**

£ [   ]

(b) **Assuming rollover relief is claimed, the gain immediately chargeable is:**

£ [   ]

(c) **The gain which Edward can rollover into the new premises is:**

£ [   ]

....

Task 14.6

On 23 May 2017 Del Ltd sold a freehold property for £145,000 which had cost originally £50,000 on 9 May 2001. On 15 April 2020 Del Ltd acquired the freehold of another property for £140,000. Rollover relief was claimed.

Indexation factor

May 2001 – May 2017   0.560

(a) **The gain on disposal in May 2017 was:**

£ [   ]

(b) **The gain available for rollover relief is:**

£ [   ]

(c) **The base cost of the property acquired in April 2020 is:**

£ [   ]

....

Task 14.7

L plc sold a plot of land.

Tick the box that correctly finishes the following statement.

If L plc wishes to claim rollover relief it must acquire a new asset between:

	✓
The start of the previous accounting period and the end of the next accounting period	
Three years before and three years after the date of the disposal	
One year before and three years after the date of the disposal	
One year before and one year after the date of the disposal	

Task 14.8

Mythili sold her 4% shareholding in D Ltd, an unquoted trading company, for £18,000 in January 2021. She had subscribed for the shares in D Ltd in June 2016 for £10,000. She also sold her 10% holding in E Ltd, a quoted trading company, for £20,000 in January 2021 having bought the shares in December 2000 for £10,000. In addition, Mythili made a gain of £20,000 on the disposal of an investment property. These were Mythili's only disposals during 2020/21 and she has brought forward capital losses of £2,000. Her taxable income in 2020/21 is £30,000.

Mythili is neither an employee of D Ltd nor E Ltd.

(a) **Using the proforma layout provided, calculate Mythili's capital gains tax liability for 2020/21. Use a 0 where no number is required and complete all the non-shaded cells.**

	Gains qualifying for 10% tax £	Other gains
Gains		
Gain on D Ltd shares		
Gain on E Ltd shares		
Gain on investment property		
Annual exempt amount		
Brought forward capital losses		

	Gains qualifying for 10% tax £	Other gains
Taxable gain		
Rate of tax applicable		
CGT payable		

(b) **State whether the following statements are true or false by ticking in the appropriate box**

	True	False
Business asset disposal relief will be available on the disposal of a 6% shareholding in L Ltd, an unquoted trading company which have been held for three years. The shareholder has worked for the company for five years.		
Investors' relief will be available on the disposal of a 1% shareholding in M Ltd, an unquoted trading company. The ordinary shares were subscribed for in September 2017 and are sold in May 2020.		
There is a lifetime limit of £10 million which applies to combined gains eligible for business asset disposal relief and investors' relief.		
The deadline for a 2020/21 claim for investors' relief is 31 January 2022.		

Answer Bank

Chapter 1 – Tax framework

Task 1.1

	Incorporated ✓	Unincorporated ✓
Sole trader		✓
Partnership		✓
Limited company	✓	

Task 1.2

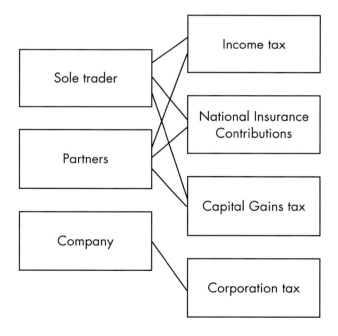

Task 1.3

	Force of law ✓	No force of law ✓
Statute law	✓	
Act of Parliament	✓	
Statutory Instrument	✓	
HMRC guidance		✓
Case Law	✓	

Task 1.4

	✓
Claiming capital allowances on a fictitious piece of equipment	
Failing to notify HMRC of a profitable trade commenced three years ago	
Obtaining tax-free interest by investing in an ISA	✓
Deciding not to declare rental income received	

Task 1.5

Ethical duties and responsibilities of an AAT accountant (Any two of the following):

Maintain client confidentiality at all times
Adopt an ethical approach and maintain an objective outlook
Give timely and constructive advice to clients
Honest and professional conduct with HMRC

Task 1.6

Tax [avoidance] is the use of loopholes in tax legislation to minimise tax liabilities.

Tax [planning] is the use of all available reliefs in the manner intended to minimise tax liabilities.

Tax [evasion] is the deliberate misleading of tax authorities to minimise tax liabilities.

Chapter 2 – Computing trading income

Task 2.1

From:	AAT student
To:	A Client
Date:	14 June
Subject:	Badges of trade

In order to decide whether a trade is being carried on the following 'badges of trade' need to be considered:

(a) **Subject matter.** When people engage in trade, they frequently do so by purchasing and re-selling objects with a view to making a profit. Objects bought for this purpose are often not the type of objects that would be bought for investment or enjoyment. This means that the subject matter of a transaction will very often indicate whether a trade is being carried on or not.

(b) **Length of ownership.** A short period of ownership is an indication of an intention to trade in a commodity.

(c) **Frequency of transactions.** Where the same type of article is repeatedly bought and sold, it will normally suggest that there is trading in that article.

(d) **Supplementary work** on or in connection with the property sold, eg modification, processing, packaging, or renovating the item sold suggests the carrying on of a trade.

(e) **Acquisition of asset.** If goods are acquired deliberately, trading may be indicated. If goods are acquired by gift or inheritance, their later sale is unlikely to constitute trading.

(f) **Profit motive.** This is usually the most important consideration though its absence does not prevent a trade being carried on if, in fact, the operation is run on commercial lines and a profit does result.

(g) **Existence of similar trading transactions or interests.** If the seller of the goods also carries out other similar trading transactions, it will normally suggest that the sale of the goods is trading.

(h) **The source of finance.** If an asset is acquired with short term finance or its disposal is necessary to repay the borrowed funds, it is likely that there is a trade.

> **(i)** **Reason for sale.** If an asset is sold for profit purposes then it is likely that a trade is being carried on. If an asset is sold for other reasons, for example a change in personal circumstances or a cash flow emergency, it would be an indicator that a trade is not being carried out.
>
> These **badges of trade** are only general indications and, in each case, all the facts must be considered before any decision can be made.

Task 2.2

	Allow ✓	Disallow and add back ✓	Not taxable so deduct ✓
Gifts of 30 bottles of wine to clients		✓	
Lease costs of a car with emissions of 150g/km		✓ (15%)	
Costs of £5,000 to repair a roof	✓		
£1,000 cost to register a patent	✓		
Accounting profit on disposal of a van			✓
£500 donation to a political party		✓	
Depreciation		✓	

Task 2.3

	£	£
Profit for the year per accounts		5,300
	Add	Deduct
Staff wages	0	0
Mr Jelly's salary (N1)	260	0
Light and heat	0	0
Motor expenses (N2) (£350 × 1/7)	50	0
Postage, stationery and telephone	0	0
Painting shop internally	0	0
Plant repairs	0	0
Stockroom extension (N3)	101	0
Provision (N4)	200	0
Donations (N2)	10	0
Advertising	0	0
Entertaining (N5)	90	0
Gifts (N6)	70	0
Legal expenses	0	0
Depreciation charge	600	0
Total net adjustments		1,381
Taxable trading profit		6,681

Notes.

1   Appropriation of profit
2   Not expenditure incurred wholly and exclusively for the purpose of trade
3   Capital items
4   Increase in general provision is disallowed
5   Entertaining expenses specifically disallowed
6   Gifts of alcohol specifically disallowed

Task 2.4

	Allow ✓	Disallow and add back ✓	Not taxable so deduct ✓
Increase in specific provision	✓		
Decrease in general provision			✓
Depreciation charge		✓	
Cocktail party held for customers		✓	
Political donation		✓	
Employees salary	✓		
Repair to factory roof	✓		

Task 2.5

Bill	Taxable trading income	Election required? (Y/N)
Expenses of £200	Nil	N
Expenses of £900	(100)	Y

With receipts not exceeding £1,000 Bill's trading assessment will be nil due to the trading allowance.

However, with expenses of £900 Bill is better off electing to disapply the trading allowance and instead choosing to calculate his trading assessment in the normal way as income minus expenses. This way he will be able to use the loss to save tax.

Belinda	Taxable trading income	Election required? (Y/N)
Expenses of £1,200	300	N
Expenses of £300	500	Y

With receipts exceeding £1,000 Belinda's trading assessment will automatically be calculated in the normal way as income minus expenses.

However, with expenses of only £300 Belinda is better off electing to deduct the trading allowance instead of expenses ie £1,500 – £1,000.

....

Task 2.6

Box 17	£25,000
Box 21	£1,760
Box 23	£1,700
Box 26	£150
Box 28	£1,650
Box 31	£30,260
Box 43	£500
Box 46	£500

....

Chapter 3 – Capital allowances

Task 3.1

	Revenue ✓	Capital ✓	Capital allowances
Purchase of machinery		✓	✓
Rent paid for premises	✓		
Insurance of premises	✓		
Repairs to roof of factory	✓		
New extension to shop		✓	
Installation of new picture window		✓	
Purchase of new car for owner		✓	✓
Legal fees relating to purchase of new factory		✓	
Payment of staff wages	✓		
Accountancy costs	✓		
Redecoration of shop	✓		

Task 3.2

	AIA £	Main pool £	Mercedes car (80%) £	Allowance £
p/e 30 April 2020				
b/f		38,500		
Additions				
14.1.19 Factory machinery	1,500,000			
30.3.19 Car			18,000	
31.3.19 Car		8,000		
2.6.19 Equipment	31,000			
Disposals				
31.12.19 Machinery		(3,000)		
AIA (note)	(1,366,667)			1,366,667
Transfer to main pool	(164,333)	164,333		
		207,833		
WDA @ 18% × 18/12		(56,115)		56,115
WDA @ 18% × 18/12			(4,860) × 80%	3,888
c/f		151,718	13,140	
Allowances				1,426,670

Note. Maximum AIA = (£200,000 × 2/12) + (£1,000,000 × 16/12) = £1,366,667

....

Task 3.3

	AIA £	FYA @ 100% £	Main pool £	Allowances £
Y/e 31 March 2021				
Additions				
6.5.20 Machinery	850,000			
6.7.20 Low emission car		8,000		
31.8.20 Car			10,500	
AIA (see note)	(800,000)			800,000
	50,000			
Transfer to main pool	(50,000)		50,000	
			60,500	
FYA @ 100%		(8,000)		8,000
		–		
WDA @ 18%			(10,890)	10,890
c/f			49,610	
Total allowances				818,890

Note. The maximum AIA for the year ended 31 March 2021 is (£1,000,000 × 9/12) + (£200,000 × 3/12) = £800,0000.

••

Task 3.4

	Main pool £	Car (1) @ 70% £	Special rate pool £	Car (2) @ 70% £	Allowances £
P/e 30 September 2020					
b/f	120,000	21,000	17,500		
Addition					
10.8.20 Car				25,000	
Disposal					
10.8.20 Car		(16,000)			
Balancing allowance		5,000 × 70%			3,500
WDA @ 18% × $\frac{6}{12}$	(10,800)				10,800
WDA @ 6% × $\frac{6}{12}$			(525)		525
WDA @ 6% × $\frac{6}{12}$				(750) × 70%	525
c/f	109,200		16,975	24,250	
Allowances					15,350

Task 3.5

	Main pool £	Special rate pool £	Allowances £
Y/e 29 February 2020			
b/f	106,000		
Addition		14,000	
WDA @ 18%	(19,080)		19,080
WDA @ 6.167%		(863)	863
c/f	86,920	13,137	
Allowances			19,943

Note. That we only ever restrict allowances for assets with private use by the proprietor (ie. sole trader or partner, NOT employees) therefore there will never be private use adjustments in a company's capital allowances workings.

The special rate pool is written down at a hybrid rate of (8% × 1/12) + (6% × 11/12) = 6.167% because one month of the period of account is before 1 April 2019 which is when the special rate was reduced from 8% to 6%, so the rate is time apportioned.

Task 3.6

Davies Ltd can claim capital allowances of £884,680

Davies Ltd – Capital allowances for year ended 31 March 2021

	AIA	Main pool	Special rate pool	SLA (1)	SLA (2)	Allowance
TWDV b/f				14,000		
Additions qualifying for AIA						
Machine	1,060,000					
AIA (See note)	(800,000)					800,000
	260,000					
To pool	(260,000)	260,000				
Computer					12,000	
Additions not qualifying for AIA						
Car			22,000			
Disposal				(12,000)		
				2,000		
Balancing allowance				(2,000)		2,000
		440,000	22,000		12,000	
WDA x 18%		(79,200)			(2,160)	81,360
WDA x 6%			(1,320)			1,320
TWDV c/f		360,800	20,680		9,840	884,680

Note. The AIA limit reduced from £1,000,000 to £200,000 on 1 January 2021. The maximum AIA is therefore (£1,000,000 × 9/12) + (£200,000 × 3/12) = £800,000

Task 3.7

XYZ plc can claim capital allowances of £614,224

	AIA	Main Pool	Special rate pool	Allowances
TWDV b/f		230,000		
Additions qualifying for AIA				
Machinery	775,000			
AIA (See note)	(550,000)			550,000
	225,000			
To main pool	(225,000)	225,000		
Additions not qualifying for the AIA				
BMW (Car)		19,000		
Audi (Car)			25,000	
Disposal				
Machine		(6,600)		
		467,400		
WDA x 18% x 9/12		(63,099)		63,099
WDA x 6% x 9/12			(1,125)	1,125
		404,301	23,875	614,224

Note. The AIA limit was reduced from £1,000,000 to £200,000 on 1 January 2021. The limit for the 9 month period ended 31 March 2021 is (£1,000,000 × 6/12) + (£200,000 × 3/12) = £550,000.

Chapter 4 – Computing corporation tax

Task 4.1

	£	£
Profit per accounts		656,980
	Add	Deduct
Depreciation charge	83,420	0
Qualifying charitable donation	1,900	0
Donation to local charity	0	0
Gifts to customers	900	0
Accountancy and audit fee	0	0
Legal fees – renewal of 20 year lease (N1)	0	0
Legal fees – issue of debenture	0	0
Repairs – knocked down wall (N2)	0	0
Initial repairs to office	12,200	0
Other expenses	0	0
Debenture interest (NTL-R income)	0	(24,700)
Bank interest (NTL-R income)	0	(4,800)
Dividends	0	(56,000)
Capital allowances	0	(13,200)
Interest payable on trading loans	0	0
Net adjustments		(280)
Taxable trading profit		656,700

Notes.

1   The costs of renewing a short lease and of obtaining loan finance for trading purposes are allowable.

2   The replacement of the wall is allowable since the whole structure is not being replaced. The repairs to the office building are not allowable, being capital in nature, as the building was not in a usable state when purchased and this was reflected in the purchase price.

Task 4.2

	Allow ✓	Disallow and add back ✓	Not taxable as trading income so deduct ✓
Dividends received from an unconnected company			✓
Profit on sale of shares			✓
Running costs of car with 20% private use by an employee	✓		
Parking fine of director		✓	
Capital allowances	✓		
Director's salary	✓		
Bank interest received			✓

....

Task 4.3

	Year to 31 December 2020 £	Five months to 31 May 2021 £
Trading profits (12:5)	352,941	147,059
Property business income (12:5)	10,800	4,500
Chargeable gain	0	3,000
Total profits	363,741	154,559
Qualifying charitable donations paid	(30,000)	(40,000)
Taxable total profits	333,741	114,559

Tutor's notes

1 Trading profits are time apportioned.

2 Property business income is time apportioned.

3 Chargeable gains are allocated to the period in which they are realised.

4 Qualifying charitable donations are allocated to the period in which they are paid.

Task 4.4

	Time apportioned ✓	Period in which arises ✓	Separate computation ✓
Capital allowances			✓
Trading income	✓		
Property income	✓		
Interest income		✓	
Chargeable gain		✓	

Task 4.5

The corporation tax payable by Rosemary Ltd for period ended 31 March 2021 is:

£	171,000

Working

	£
Trading profits	600,000
Property business income	300,000
Taxable total profits	900,000

Note. Dividends are not included as part of taxable total profits.

FY20	£
£900,000 × 19%	171,000

Chapter 5 – Taxing unincorporated businesses

Task 5.1

Her first tax year is:

2018/19

Her taxable profits in her first tax year of trading are:

£	6,188

Her taxable profits in her second tax year of trading are:

£	24,750

Her taxable profits in her third tax year of trading are:

£	24,750

Overlap profits are:

£	22,688

Working

Taxable profits

Tax year	Basis period	Taxable profits £
2018/19	(1.1.19 – 5.4.19) £33,000 × $^{3}/_{16}$ =	**6,188**
2019/20	(6.4.19 – 5.4.20) £33,000 × $^{12}/_{16}$ =	**24,750**
2020/21	(1.5.19 – 30.4.20) £33,000 × $^{12}/_{16}$ =	**24,750**

Overlap profits

The profits taxed twice are those for the period 1 May 2019 to 5 April 2020:

$^{11}/_{16}$ × £33,000

Task 5.2

Mr Phone's basis period for 2018/19 runs from:

| 01/07/2018 |

to:

| 05/04/2019 |

Mr Phone's basis period for 2019/20 runs from:

| 01/07/2018 |

to:

| 30/06/2019 |

His taxable profits in his second tax year of trading are:

| £ | 23,500 |

Overlap profits are:

| £ | 19,500 |

Working

Tax year	Basis period	Taxable profits £
2018/19	Actual	
	1 July 2018 to 5 April 2019	
	(9/11 × £22,000)	18,000
2019/20	First 12 months	
	1 July 2018 to 30 June 2019	
	£22,000 + (1/12 × £18,000)	23,500
2020/21	(CYB)	
	Year ended 31 May 2020	18,000

	£
Overlap period is 1 July 2018 to 5 April 2019	18,000
and 1 June 2019 to 30 June 2019	
(1/12 × £18,000)	1,500
	19,500

Task 5.3

Mr Mug's final tax year is:

2020/21

Mr Mug's penultimate tax year is:

2019/20

His taxable profits in his final tax year of trading are:

£ 11,000

Working

		£
2020/21	1 May 2019 to 31 December 2020 (16,000 + 4,000)	20,000
	Less overlap relief	(9,000)
		11,000

Note. Year ended 30 April 2019 was assessed in 2019/20.

Task 5.4

Jackie's first tax year is:

2016/17

Her taxable profits in her first tax year of trading are:

£	13,200

Jackie's second tax year is:

2017/18

Her taxable profits in her second tax year of trading are:

£	14,400

Jackie's final tax year is:

2020/21

Her taxable profits in her final tax year of trading are:

£	300

Over the life of her business Jackie is assessed on total profits of:

£	48,240

Working

Tax year	Basis period	Taxable profits £
2016/17	First year – 1.5.16 to 5.4.17	
	11/15 × £18,000	13,200
2017/18	Second year 12 months to 31.7.17 (1.8.16 – 31.7.17)	
	12/15 × £18,000	14,400
2018/19	Third year y/e 31.7.18	11,700
2019/20	y/e 31.7.19	8,640

Tax year	Basis period	Taxable profits £
2020/21	Y/e 31.7.20	4,800
	P/e 28.2.21	5,100
		9,900
	Less overlap profits	(9,600)
		300

Overlap profits

Overlap period is 1 August 2016 to 5 April 2017, ie 8/15 × £18,000 = £9,600

....

Task 5.5

The year of change for Matilda's business is:

2019/20

Her basis period for the tax year 2018/19 is:

1/4/18 – 31/3/19

Her basis period for the tax year 2019/20 is:

1/1/19 – 31/12/19

Her basis period for the tax year 2020/21 is:

1/1/20 – 31/12/20

....

Chapter 6 – Partnerships

Task 6.1

	Total £	Fimbo £	Florrie £	Pom £
12 months to 31 December 2019				
Salary	5,000	5,000	0	0
Share of profits	5,000	3,000	2,000	0
Total for year	10,000	8,000	2,000	0
12 months to 31 December 2020				
Salary	5,000	5,000	0	0
Share of profits	15,000	9,000	6,000	0
Total for year	20,000	14,000	6,000	0
12 months to 31 December 2021				
Salary	6,500	6,500	0	0
Share of profits	18,500	6,167	6,167	6,166
Total for year	25,000	12,667	6,167	6,166

Task 6.2

(a)

	Total £	John £	Paul £	George £
Period ended 31 July 2018				
Division of profits	24,300	9,720	7,290	7,290
Year ended 31 July 2019				
Division of profits	16,200	6,480	4,860	4,860
Year ended 31 July 2020				
Division of profits	14,900	5,960	4,470	4,470

(b)

	John £	Paul £	George £
2017/18	4,166	3,124	3,124
2018/19	12,420	9,315	9,315
2019/20	6,480	4,860	4,860
2020/21	5,960	4,470	4,470

Working

	John £	Paul £	George £
2017/18			
1 January 2018 – 5 April 2018			
3/7 × £(9,720/7,290/7,290)	4,166	3,124	3,124
2018/19			
(1 January 2018 to 31 December 2018)			
1 January 2018 to 31 July 2018	9,720	7,290	7,290
1 August 2018 to 31 December 2018			
5/12 × £(6,480/4,860/4,860)	2,700	2,025	2,025
	12,420	9,315	9,315
2019/20			
Year ended 31 July 2019	6,480	4,860	4,860
2020/21			
Year ended 31 July 2020	5,960	4,470	4,470

Task 6.3

Year ended 31 December 2020	Total £	Strange £	Pavin £	Lehman £
To 31 July 2020				
Salaries (15,000/5000 × 7/12)	11,667	8,750	2,917	0
Interest on capital (20,000/10,000 × 5% × 7/12)	875	583	292	0
Division of profits (48,000 × 7/12 – 11,667 – 875)	15,458	7,729	5,153	2,576
To 31 December 2020				
Salary (20,000 × 5/12)	8,333	8,333	0	0
Division of profits (48,000 × 5/12 – 8,333)	11,667	4,667	4,667	2,333
Total for year ended 31 December 2020	48,000	30,062	13,029	4,909

Task 6.4

Year ended 31 May 2020	Total £	Bob £	Annie £	John £
To 31 January 2020				
Salaries	30,000	10,000	10,000	10,000
Division of profits	30,000	15,000	7,500	7,500
To 31 May 2020				
Salaries	10,000	0	5,000	5,000
Division of profits	20,000	0	10,000	10,000
Total for year ended 31 May 2020	90,000	25,000	32,500	32,500

Task 6.5

Page 6

Box 1	01/01/20
Box 2	31/12/20
Box 3	Retail – designer dresses
Box 11	36,000
Box 13	8,000
Box 6	Anne Curtis
Box 11	18,000
Box 13	4,000

Working

Tax adjusted trading profit for the partnership is:

	£
Revenue	125,000
Cost of goods	(75,000)
Rental	(12,000)
Admin	(1,700)
Accountancy	(650)
Goods for own use	1,550
AIA on sewing machine	(1,200)
	36,000

Chapter 7 – National insurance

Task 7.1

The Class 2 NIC liability for 2020/21 is:

£	158	.	60

The Class 4 NIC liability for 2020/21 is:

£	299	.	70

The total NIC liability for 2020/21 is:

£	458	.	30

Working

	£
Profits	12,830
Less lower profits limit	(9,500)
Excess	3,330

Class 4 NICs (9% × £3,330)	=	£299.70
Class 2 NICs = £3.05 × 52	=	£158.60
Total NICs £(299.70+158.60)	=	**£458.30**

Task 7.2

The Class 2 NIC liability for **2020/21** is:

£	158	.	60

The Class 4 NIC liability for **2020/21** is:

£	3,805	.	00

The total NIC liability for **2020/21** is:

£	3,963	.	60

Working

	£
Upper profits limit	50,000
Less: lower profits limit	(9,500)
Excess	40,500

	£
Class 4 NICs (9% × £40,500)	3,645.00
+ 2% × £(58,000 – 50,000)	160.00
	3805.00

Class 2 NICs = £3.05 × 52   =   £158.60

Total NICs £(3,805.00+ 158.60)   =   **£3963.60**

••

Task 7.3

The Class 2 NIC liability for 2020/21 is:

£	0	.	0

The Class 4 NIC liability for 2020/21 is:

£	0	.	0

The total NIC liability for 2020/21 is:

£	0	.	0

As Raj's trading profits are below the lower profits limit, there is no liability to Class 4 NICs. There is also no liability to Class 2 NICs because his profits are below the small profits threshold of £6,475.

••

Task 7.4

The Class 2 NIC liability for 2020/21 is:

£	158	.	60

The Class 4 NIC liability for 2020/21 is:

£	4,245	.	00

The total NIC liability for 2020/21 is:

£	4,403	.	60

Working

Class 2 = £3.05 × 52 = £158.60

		£
Class 4	£(50,000 – 9,500) × 9% (main)	3,645.00
	£(80,000 – 50,000) × 2% (additional)	600.00
		4,245.00

Total NICs £(4,245.00 + 158.60) = **£4403.60**

....

Task 7.5

(a) The share of profits taxable on Paula for 2020/21 is:

£	14,000

Working

Share of profits for y/e 31.12.21 is £280,000 × 20% = £56,000
Basis period for 2020/21 = 1.1.21 to 5.4.21 (3/12 × £56,000 = £14,000)

and for 2021/22 is:

£	56,000

Working

Basis period for 2021/22 = 1.1.21 to 31.12.21

and the overlap profits to carry forward are:

£	14,000

Working

1.1.21 to 5.4.21 (3/12 × £56,000 = £14,000)

(b) The Class 4 National Insurance Contributions payable by Paula for 2020/21 are:

£	405	.	00

Working

£(14,000 – 9,500) = £4,500 × 9%

Chapter 8 – Losses

Task 8.1

	2018/19 £	2019/20 £	2020/21 £	2021/22 £
Trading profits	12,000	0	8,000	14,000
Trading loss offset against future year	0	0	(8,000)	(3,600)
Property income	10,400	11,000	11,000	11,000
Trading loss offset against current year	0	(11,000)	0	0
Trading loss offset against previous year	(22,400)	0	0	0
Net income	0	0	11,000	21,400

Task 8.2

	✓
True	
False	✓

An individual cannot restrict a claim to set a trading loss against total income in order to have enough net income to use his personal allowance – the loss must be set-off as far as possible even if this means that the personal allowance is not available.

Task 8.3

	✓
True	
False	✓

An individual does not have to make a trading loss claim against total income in the tax year of the loss before making a claim to set the loss against total income in the preceding year – a claim can be made for either year or both years, and in any order.

Task 8.4

	✓
True	✓
False	

An individual can only carry a trading loss forward against trading income of the same trade.

Task 8.5

(a)

	Year ended 31 March		
	2019 £	2020 £	2021 £
Trading profits	62,000	20,000	0
NTLR income	1,200	600	1,200
Total profits	63,200	20,600	1,200
Current period loss relief	0	0	(1,200)
Carry back loss relief	0	(20,600)	0
Total profits after loss relief	63,200	0	0
Qualifying charitable donation	(100)	0	0
Taxable total profits	63,100	0	0

(b) The trading loss available to carry forward at 31 March 2021 is:

£	61,200

Working

(£83,000 – £1,200 – £20,600)

Task 8.6

(a)

	Year ended 30.6.18 £	9 months to 31.3.19 £	Year ended 31.3.20 £	Year ended 31.3.21 £
Trading profits	6,200	4,320	0	53,000
NTLR income	80	240	260	200
Property income	1,420	1,440	1,600	1,500
Chargeable gains	0	7,680	0	0
Total profits	7,700	13,680	1,860	54,700
Current period loss relief	0	0	(1,860)	0
Carry back loss relief	(1,925)	(13,680)	0	0
Carry forward loss relief				(54,700)
Total profits after loss relief	5,775	0	0	0
Qualifying charitable donation	(1,000)	0	0	0
Taxable total profits	4,775	0	0	0

Tutor's note. The loss can be carried back to set against profits arising in the previous 12 months. This means that the set-off in the y/e 30.6.18 is restricted to $3/12 \times £7,700 = £1,925$. When a loss is carried forward, a claim must be made to specify the amount of loss relieved.

(b) The trading loss available to carry forward at 31 March 2021 is:

£	27,835

Working

(£100,000 – £1,860 – £13,680 – £1,925 – £54,700)

(c) The capital loss available to carry forward at 31 March 2021 is:

£	9,423

Task 8.7

	✓
True	✓
False	

A company must offset its trading loss against total profits in the loss-making period before carrying the loss back.

Task 8.8

	✓
True	✓
False	

If a company carries a trading loss forward, the company can choose how much of the loss is to be set against total profits so as not to waste any qualifying donations.

Task 8.9

	✓
True	
False	✓

A company can set-off a capital loss against capital gains only.

Chapter 9 – Self assessment for individuals

Task 9.1

	✓
31 January 2022	✓
5 April 2022	
31 October 2021	
31 December 2021	

Task 9.2

	✓
The full amount of £20,500 will be paid on 31 January 2022.	
Payments on account based on the estimated 2020/21 liability will be made on 31 January and 31 July 2021, with the balance payable on 31 January 2022.	
Payments on account of £10,250 will be made on 31 January and 31 July 2021 with nothing due on 31 January 2022.	
Payments on account of £7,250 will be made on 31 January and 31 July 2021, with the balance of £6,000 being paid on 31 January 2022.	✓

Task 9.3

	✓
100%	
50%	✓
35%	
15%	

Task 9.4

	✓
True	✓
False	

The return is filed less than 3 months after the due filing date.

Task 9.5

	✓
True	✓
False	

The penalty for failure to keep records is £3,000 per tax year or accounting period.

Task 9.6

	✓
True	
False	✓

Penalties for late payment do not apply to payments on account.

Chapter 10 – Self assessment for companies

Task 10.1

Instalment	Due date	Amount due £
1	14/10/2020	125,000
2	14/01/2021	125,000
3	14/04/2021	125,000
4	14/07/2021	125,000

Task 10.2

	True ✓	False ✓
A company with a period of account ending on 31 March 2021 must keep its records until 31 March 2023.		✓ (until 31 March 2027)
The due date for payment of CGT for 2020/21 is 31 January 2022.	✓	
An individual who becomes chargeable to income tax in 2020/21 must notify HMRC by 31 October 2021.		✓ (by 5 October 2021)
A large company will not have to pay corporation tax by instalments if it has profits not exceeding £10m and was not large in the previous accounting period.	✓	
A company which is not large (for corporation tax purposes) must pay its corporation tax by nine months and one day after the end of its accounting period.	✓	

Task 10.3

The corporation tax return must be filed by:

| 28/02/2022 |

The corporation tax return must be filed by:

| 30/06/2021 |

Task 10.4

A company must keep its accounting records for | six | years. Failure to

do so may incur a penalty of | £ | 3,000 |.

Task 10.5

The fact that Fred derives nearly all of his income from one client, and uses that client's equipment implies that IR35 may apply, as they are aspects of engagement generally associated with permanent employment.

The fact that Fred can provide a replacement to perform his duties would suggest that IR35 does not apply.

Fred will be taxed on a deemed employment charge.

This will be subject to income tax and NICs.

The dividends he is currently extracting from Fred Services Ltd are not subject to NICs.

There are fewer expenses deductible from the deemed employment charge than from a company's trading profits.

Task 10.6

The amount which is deductible as a trading expense is £ 115,000 .
(£50,000 × 230%)

If this resulted in a loss, the loss could be surrendered in exchange for a tax credit at the rate of 14.5 %.

Chapter 11 – Chargeable gains – the basics

Task 11.1

For the gain on the disposal of a capital asset to be a chargeable gain there must be a chargeable | disposal | of a chargeable | asset | by a chargeable | person |.

Task 11.2

Item	Chargeable ✓	Exempt ✓
Wasting chattel with useful life of 25 years		✓
Disposal of half the holding of a plot of land	✓	
Car used for business purposes		✓

Task 11.3

	✓
£33,300	✓
£38,300	
£45,600	
£56,600	

Working

	£
Proceeds of sale	90,600
Less cost	(40,000)
Less enhancement expenditure	(5,000)
Chargeable gain	45,600
Less annual exempt amount	(12,300)
Taxable gain	33,300

Task 11.4

(a) George's capital gains tax liability for 2020/21 is:

£	828

Working

	£
Chargeable gains	20,000
Less allowable losses	(3,560)
Net chargeable gains	16,440
Less annual exempt amount	(12,300)
Taxable gains	4,140
CGT @ 20%	**£828**

(b) George's capital gains tax liability is payable by:

31 January 2022

Task 11.5

Jack would pay capital gains tax at:

20%

Gains are subject to capital gains tax at 10% (for basic rate taxpayers) and 20% (for higher and additional rate taxpayers).

Task 11.6

The amount of the loss Graham will use in 2020/21 is:

£	5,200

Note. Current year losses cannot be restricted in order to get the benefit of the annual exempt amount.

Working

	£
Chargeable gains	15,000
Less allowable losses	(5,200)
Net chargeable gains	9,800
Less annual exempt amount	(12,300)
Taxable gains	0

....

Task 11.7

Gayle's capital gains tax liability for 2020/21 is:

£	1,260

Working

	£
Chargeable gains (£5,000 + £18,100)	23,100
Less allowable losses	(2,000)
Net chargeable gains	21,100
Less annual exempt amount	(12,300)
Taxable gains	8,800

CGT payable

	£
£5,000 @ 10%	500
£3,800 @ 20%	760
	1,260

....

Task 11.8

Gerry's capital gains tax liability for 2020/21 is:

£	1,811

Working

	£
Chargeable gains	27,100
Less annual exempt amount	(12,300)
Taxable gains	14,800

CGT	£
£11,495 (W) @ 10%	1,150
£3,305 @ 20%	661
	1,811
(W) Unused basic rate band is £37,500 – £26,005 = £11,495	

Task 11.9

The losses to carry forward to 2021/22 are:

£	3,000

Working

(5,000 – 2,000)

	£
Gains	20,900
Losses	(6,600)
	14,300
Less annual exempt amount	(12,300)
	2000
Losses b/f	(2,000)
Taxable gains	Nil

Task 11.10

The maximum allowable loss carried forward to 2021/22 will be:

£	11,400

Working

Tax year	2018/19 £	2019/20 £	2020/21 £
Gains	2,000	4,000	14,900
Losses	(14,000)	(2,000)	(2,000)
Net gain/(loss)	(12,000)	2,000	12,900
Less annual exempt amount	0	(2,000)	(12,300)
Loss b/f			(600)
Chargeable gain	0	0	0
Loss c/f	(12,000)	(12,000)	(11,400)

The loss brought forward in 2020/21 is used after the annual exempt amount, whereas the current year losses in each year are offset before the AEA.

....

Task 11.11

	£
Proceeds	230,000
Less cost	(160,000)
Unindexed gain	70,000
Less indexation allowance 0.535 × £160,000 (restricted)	(70,000)
Chargeable gain/allowable loss	0

....

Task 11.12

	£
Proceeds	180,000
Less: cost	(100,000)
enhancement expenditure	(25,000)
Unindexed gain	55,000
Less: indexation allowance on cost 0.407 × £100,000	(40,700)
indexation allowance on enhancement 0.280 × £25,000	(7,000)
Chargeable gain	7,300

Task 11.13

	✓
True	
False	✓

Individuals are entitled to an annual exempt amount but not companies.

Chapter 12 – Further aspects of chargeable gains

Task 12.1

(a) The cost of the land sold is:

£	120,000

Working

$$\frac{240,000}{240,000 + 60,000} \times £150,000$$

(b) The gain on sale is:

£	117,000

Working

	£
Disposal proceeds	240,000
Less: disposal costs	(3,000)
Net proceeds	237,000
Less: cost	(120,000)
Chargeable gain	**117,000**

Task 12.2

Her chargeable gain on sale is:

	✓
£2,300	
£2,000	
£2,500	
£1,700	✓

Working

	£
Gross proceeds	7,500
Less costs of sale	(300)
Net proceeds	7,200
Less cost	(5,500)
Chargeable gain	1,700
Gain cannot exceed 5/3 × £(7,500 – 6,000)	2,500

Task 12.3

Mark's allowable loss is:

£	3,500

Working

	£
Deemed proceeds	6,000
Less costs of sale £(4,500 × 100/90) = £5,000 × 10%	(500)
Net proceeds	5,500
Less cost	(9,000)
Allowable loss	**(3,500)**

Task 12.4

	✓
True	
False	✓

The proceeds are less than £6,000 so the gain is exempt.

Task 12.5

John's chargeable gains (before the annual exempt amount) for 2020/21 are:

	✓
£45,000	✓
£30,000	
£32,700	
£17,700	

The gain on the disposal to John's brother is £(60,000 – 15,000) = £45,000. The loss on the disposal to John's daughter can only be set against disposals to that connected person.

....

Task 12.6

	✓
True	✓
False	

Disposals to connected persons are deemed to be at market value.

....

Task 12.7

(a) The cost of the two offices disposed of is:

£	76,087

Working

$$£250,000 \times \frac{140,000}{140,000 + 320,000}$$

(b) The chargeable gain arising on the disposal is:

£	23,511

Working

	£
Proceeds	140,000
Less cost	(76,087)
	63,913
Less IA	
0.531 × £76,087	(40,402)
Chargeable gain	**23,511**

Task 12.8

	£
Proceeds	8,000
Disposal costs	(500)
Cost of acquisition	(4,500)
Indexation allowance (4,500 × 0.277)	(1,247)
Gain	1,753
Gain using chattel marginal relief 5/3 (8,000 – 6,000)	3,333
Chargeable gain (lower of actual gain and marginal relief)	1,753

Chapter 13 – Share disposals

Task 13.1

His net gain on sale is:

£	9,800

Working

Match acquisition in next 30 days first

	£
Proceeds of sale £20,000 × 1,000/5,000	4,000
Less cost	(4,200)
Loss	(200)

Then match with share pool

	£
Proceeds of sale £20,000 × 4,000/5,000	16,000
Less cost £9,000 × 4,000/6,000	(6,000)
Gain	10,000

Task 13.2

Share pool

	No. of shares	Cost £
10 February 2001	12,000	18,000
20 September 2008 Bonus 1:4	3,000	0
Total before disposal	15,000	18,000
15 March 2021 Disposal	(2,000)	(2,400)
c/f	13,000	15,600

Gain on sale

	£
Proceeds	8,000
Less cost	(2,400)
Gain	5,600

Task 13.3

Share pool

	No. of shares	Cost £
9 December 2001: purchase	12,000	4,400
12 October 2005 Rights 1:3 @ £5	4,000	20,000
Total before disposal	16,000	24,400
4 November 2020 Disposal	(8,000)	(12,200)
c/f	8,000	12,200

Gains on sale

	£	£
Next 30 days		
Proceeds (2,000/10,000 × 60,000)	12,000	
Cost	(11,500)	
Gain/(loss)		500
Share pool		
Proceeds (8,000/10,000 × 60,000)	48,000	
Cost	(12,200)	
Gain/(loss)		35,800
Total gain/(loss)		36,300

Task 13.4

FA 1985 pool

	No. of shares	Original cost £	Indexed cost £
September 2001			
Acquisition	5,000	10,000	10,000
October 2004			
Indexed rise 0.080 × £10,000			800
Rights 1:5 @ £5	1,000	5,000	5,000
	6,000	15,000	15,800
August 2006			
Indexed rise 0.056 × £15,800			885
Acquisition	14,000	84,000	84,000
	20,000	99,000	100,685
January 2021			
Indexed rise 0.396 × £100,685			39,871
			140,556
Sale (99,000/140,556 × 18,000/20,000)	(18,000)	(89,100)	(126,500)
c/f	2,000	9,900	14,056

Gain

	£
Proceeds	155,000
Less cost	(89,100)
	65,900
Less indexation allowance £(126,500 – 89,100)	(37,400)
Chargeable gain	28,500

Task 13.5

FA 1985 pool

	No. of shares	Cost £	Indexed cost £
26 May 1995			
Acquisition	4,000	24,000	24,000
30 June 1996 Bonus issue (1/2 × 4,000)	2,000		
24 October 2003			
Indexed rise 0.221 × £24,000			5,304
Acquisition	5,000	27,500	27,500
c/f	11,000	51,500	56,804
25 May 2020			
Indexed rise 0.523 × £56,804			29,708
			86,512
Disposal	(11,000)	(51,500)	(86,512)
c/f	0	0	0

Gain

	£
Proceeds	78,200
Less cost	(51,500)
	26,700
Less indexation allowance £(86,512 – 51,500)	(35,012)
Gain	Nil

Task 13.6

	✓
True	✓
False	

Indexation allowance on rights issue shares runs from the date of the rights issue even though the rights issue shares are treated as having been acquired at the time of the original acquisition to which they relate.

Chapter 14 – Reliefs for chargeable gains

Task 14.1

	£	£
Proceeds of goodwill	50,000	
Less cost	0	
Gain/(loss) on goodwill		50,000
Proceeds of shop	90,000	
Less cost	(80,000)	
Gain/(loss) on shop		10,000
Proceeds of warehouse	130,000	
Less cost	(150,000)	
Gain/(loss) on warehouse		(20,000)
Net gains eligible for business asset disposal relief		40,000
Less annual exempt amount		(12,300)
Taxable gains		27,700
CGT payable		2,770

Task 14.2

	✓
True	✓
False	

The lifetime limit of gains eligible for business asset disposal relief is £1,000,000.

Task 14.3

The taxable gain arising on the sale of the Blue Ltd shares is:

£ | 137,700

Working

	£	£
Proceeds		200,000
Less cost	65,000	
Less gain rolled over	(15,000)	
		(50,000)
Chargeable gain		150,000
Less annual exempt amount		(12,300)
Taxable gain		**137,700**

Task 14.4

(a) Fran's chargeable gain on her disposal is:

£ | 0

Working

	£
Proceeds (MV) June 2020	500,000
Less cost	(75,000)
Gain	425,000
Less gift relief	(425,000)
Gain left in charge	**0**

(b) Anna's chargeable gain on her disposal is:

£	445,000

Working

	£	£
Proceeds July 2021		520,000
Cost (MV)	500,000	
Less gift relief gain (from above)	(425,000)	
Base cost		(75,000)
Chargeable gain		**445,000**

Task 14.5

(a) Edward's gain on the disposal before rollover relief is:

£	65,000

Working

	£
Proceeds	125,000
Less cost	(60,000)
Gain	**65,000**

(b) Assuming rollover relief is claimed, the gain immediately chargeable is:

£	1,500

Proceeds not re-invested (£125,000 – £123,500)

(c) The gain which Edward can rollover into the new premises is:

| £ | £63,500 |

Working

	£
Gain	65,000
Less immediately chargeable	(1,500)
Gain rolled-over against new premises	63,500

....

Task 14.6

(a) The gain on disposal in May 2017 was:

| £ | 67,000 |

Working

	£
Proceeds	145,000
Less cost	(50,000)
	95,000
Less indexation allowance 0.560 × £50,000	(28,000)
Chargeable gain	**67,000**

(b) The gain available for rollover relief is:

| £ | 62,000 |

Working

	£
Gain	67,000
Less chargeable in 2017	
Proceeds not reinvested = £(145,000 – 140,000)	(5,000)
Gain available for rollover relief	**62,000**

(c) The base cost of the property acquired in April 2020 is:

£	78,000

Working

	£
Cost of new property	140,000
Less gain rolled over	(62,000)
Base cost of new property	**78,000**

Task 14.7

	✓
The start of the previous accounting period and the end of the next accounting period	
Three years before and three years after the date of the disposal	
One year before and three years after the date of the disposal	✓
One year before and one year after the date of the disposal	

Task 14.8

(a)

	Gains qualifying for 10% tax £	Other gains
Gains		
Gain on D Ltd shares (£18,000-£10,000)	8,000	0
Gain on E Ltd shares (£20,000-£10,000)	0	10,000
Gain on investment property	0	20,000
Annual exempt amount	0	(12,300)
Brought forward capital losses	0	(2,000)

	Gains qualifying for 10% tax £	Other gains
Taxable gain	8,000	15,700
Rate of tax applicable	10%	20%
CGT payable	800	3,140

(b)

	True	False
Business asset disposal relief will be available on the disposal of a 6% shareholding in L Ltd, an unquoted trading company which have been held for three years. The shareholder has worked for the company for five years - This statement correctly meets the conditions for BADR. See reference material available in your assessment for the conditions.	✓	
Investors' relief will be available on the disposal of a 1% shareholding in M Ltd, an unquoted trading company. The ordinary shares were subscribed for in September 2017 and are sold in May 2020 - This statement is false as the shares have not been held for three years. See the reference material for conditions.		✓
There is a lifetime limit of £10 million which applies to combined gains eligible for business asset disposal relief and investors' relief - This statement is false as there is a separate limit for each of business asset disposal relief and investors' relief rather than a combined limit.		✓
The deadline for a 2020/21 claim for investors' relief is 31 January 2022 – The deadline for the claim is in 2023 not 2022. See reference material for the deadline.		✓

AAT AQ2016
ASSESSMENT 1
Business Tax

Time allowed: 2 hours

You are advised to attempt the AAT practice/sample assessment 1 online from the AAT website. This will ensure you are prepared for how the assessment will be presented on the AAT's system when you attempt the real assessment. Please access the assessment using the address below:

https://www.aat.org.uk/training/study-support/search

AAT AQ2016
ASSESSMENT 2
Business Tax

You are advised to attempt the assessment 2 online from the AAT website. This will ensure you are prepared for how the assessment will be presented on the AAT's system when you attempt the real assessment. Please access the assessment using the address below:

https://www.aat.org.uk/training/study-support/search

AAT AQ2016 PRACTICE ASSESSMENT 2

BPP PRACTICE ASSESSMENT 1 BUSINESS TAX

Time allowed: 2 hours

Business Tax (BSTX)
BPP practice assessment 1

In the live assessment you will have access to the Tax tables and reference material which have been reproduced at the back of this Question Bank. Please use them whilst completing this practice assessment so that you are familiar with their content.

Task 1 (10 marks)

The statement of profit or loss for George Checkers shows the following:

	£	£
Gross profit		396,550
General expenses (see notes below)	85,480	
Irrecoverable debts (see notes below)	585	
Motor expenses (see notes below)	7,880	
Wages and salaries	54,455	
Depreciation charge	21,080	
		(169,480)
Profit for the year		227,070

Notes.

General expenses include	£
Gifts to customers – Christmas cakes costing £4.50 each	1,350
Building a new wall around car park	2,200

Irrecoverable debts are made up of:	£
Trade debts written-off	350
Increase in general provision	400
Trade debts recovered	(165)
	585

Motor expenses are made up of:	Private usage %	Annual expense £
George	25	6,600
Salesman	20	1,280
Capital allowances computed to be:		15,000

(a) **Complete the computation provided below. Fill in all unshaded boxes. Do not use minus signs or brackets to show negative numbers.** **(6 marks)**

	£
Profit for the year per accounts	
Disallowed items added back	
[A] ▼	
[B] ▼	
[C] ▼	
[D] ▼	
[E] ▼	
Total to add back	
Allowed items deducted	
[F] ▼	
Adjusted trading profits	

Picklist for A to E:

Gifts to customers – cakes
New wall
Trade debts written-off
Increase in general provision
Private motor expenses – George
Private motor expenses – salesman
Depreciation charge

Picklist for F:

Trade debts recovered
Capital allowances

(b) **For the following items, tick the correct treatment when computing the adjusted trading profits:** **(4 marks)**

	Allowed ✓	Disallowed – add back ✓	Disallowed – deduct ✓
Purchase of raw materials			
Private use of vehicle by an employee			
Purchase of delivery van			
Interest received on business bank account			

Task 2 (14 marks)

(a) Jude and Kelly have been in partnership for many years making up accounts to 30 September each year. They share profits 3:1 respectively.

On 1 July 2020, Liam joined the partnership. It was agreed that Liam would be paid a salary of £6,000 per year and that profits would be shared 2:2:1 for Jude, Kelly and Liam.

For the year ended 30 September 2020, the partnership trading profit was £54,000.

Show the division of profits between the partners for the year ended 30 September 2020 in the table below. Fill in all unshaded boxes and add a 0 (zero) if necessary. **(10 marks)**

	Jude £	Kelly £	Liam £
Period to: (Insert dates as: xx/xx/xxxx)			
Division of profits			
Period to: (Insert dates as: xx/xx/xxxx)			
Salary			
Division of profits			
Total profit for y/e 30/09/2020			

(b) The following accounts have been prepared for a sole trader: **(4 marks)**

	£
Y/e 30/06/2019	45,000
Y/e 30/06/2020	42,000
Period to: 30/11/2020	15,000

The trade ceased on 30 November 2020 and overlap profits from commencement were £9,500.

(i) **The penultimate tax year is: (insert as xxxx/xx)**

(ii) **The final tax year is: (insert as xxxx/xx)**

(iii) **The profits for the penultimate year of trade are:**

£

(iv) **The profits for the final year of trade are:**

£

Task 3 (12 Marks)

Mr Wish commenced trade on 1 July 2020. He made up his first set of accounts for six months to 31 December 2020 and yearly from then on.

The following fixed asset information is available for his first 18 months of trade:

Date	Additions	Cost £
1 July 20	New plant and machinery.	530,400
15 July 20	A car with CO_2 emissions of 100g/km. Mr Wish used this car 75% of the time for business purposes.	16,000
2 Mar 21	A car with CO_2 emissions of 170g/km. This car is used 20% of the time by a salesman for private purposes.	28,000
2 July 21	A new car for Mr Wish with CO_2 emissions of 50g/km. Mr Wish used this car 75% of the time for business purposes.	17,500

Date	Disposals	Proceeds £
15 Dec 20	Plant purchased for £32,000.	18,000
1 July 21	Mr Wish's car bought on 15 July 18.	15,300

Calculate the capital allowances for Mr Wish for the six month period ended 31 December 2020 and the year ended 31 December 2021. Show the balances to carry forward to the next accounting period.
(12 marks)

	£	£	£	£	£	£	£

Task 4 (9 marks)

Isla Grace has carried on in business for many years as an osteopath making up accounts to 31 March each year.

The following information is relevant to her period of account to 31 March 2021:

	£
Revenue	127,000
Cost of materials used in her practice	15,000
Running costs of van for transporting treatment table (70% business)	8,500
Insurance	5,900
Office costs	15,600
Electricity	1,200
Accountancy	1,500
Bad debt written off	110
Equipment purchased	2,500

Using this information, complete the self employment page
(9 marks)

Business expenses
Please read the 'Self-employment (full) notes' before filling in this section.

Total expenses	Disallowable expenses
If your annual turnover was below £85,000, you may just put your total expenses in box 31	Use this column if the figures in boxes 17 to 30 include disallowable amounts
17 Cost of goods bought for resale or goods used £ · 0 0	**32** £ · 0 0
18 Construction industry – payments to subcontractors £ · 0 0	**33** £ · 0 0
19 Wages, salaries and other staff costs £ · 0 0	**34** £ · 0 0
20 Car, van and travel expenses £ · 0 0	**35** £ · 0 0
21 Rent, rates, power and insurance costs £ · 0 0	**36** £ · 0 0
22 Repairs and maintenance of property and equipment £ · 0 0	**37** £ · 0 0
23 Phone, fax, stationery and other office costs £ · 0 0	**38** £ · 0 0
24 Advertising and business entertainment costs £ · 0 0	**39** £ · 0 0
25 Interest on bank and other loans £ · 0 0	**40** £ · 0 0
26 Bank, credit card and other financial charges £ · 0 0	**41** £ · 0 0
27 Irrecoverable debts written off £ · 0 0	**42** £ · 0 0
28 Accountancy, legal and other professional fees £ · 0 0	**43** £ · 0 0
29 Depreciation and loss or profit on sale of assets £ · 0 0	**44** £ · 0 0
30 Other business expenses £ · 0 0	**45** £ · 0 0
31 Total expenses (total of boxes 17 to 30) £ · 0 0	**46** Total disallowable expenses (total of boxes 32 to 45) £ · 0 0

SA103F 2021   Page SEF 2

(Adapted from HMRC, 2020)

148

Task 5 (5 marks)

(a) A company made up accounts to 31 December 2019. It decides to make up its next set of accounts to 31 March 2021.

Identify how the company will deal with its capital allowances in the long period of account. Tick ONE box. (1 mark)

	✓
One computation from 1 January 2020 to 31 March 2021	
Two computations: one from 1 January 2020 to 31 March 2020 and one from 1 April 2020 to 31 March 2021	
Two computations: one from 1 January 2020 to 31 December 2020 and one from 1 January 2021 to 31 March 2021	
It can deal with the computation for whatever period the company chooses	

(b) Abbey Ltd has the following information for the year ended 31 March 2021.

The adjusted trading profit, after deducting capital allowances of £37,430, was £620,843.

The company sold a piece of investment land in December 2020 realising a gain of £67,817.

Abbey Ltd has one wholly owned subsidiary. **(3 marks)**

(i) **Abbey Ltd's taxable total profits are:**

£

(ii) **The corporation tax payable for the year ended 31 March 2021 is:**

£

(iii) **The due date for payment is: (insert as xx/xx/xxxx)**

(c) T Ltd, a large company, has a corporation tax liability of £600,000 in respect of its accounting year ended 31 December 2020.

Identify the date the company will be required to pay its FINAL instalment of the liability. Tick ONE box. (1 mark)

	✓
14 October 2020	
14 January 2021	
14 April 2021	
1 October 2021	

Task 6 (11 marks)

Mina is a client of yours. She has tax payable for 2020/21 of £4,225, but was not required to make any payments on account for this tax year.

Mina is looking for advice about when she needs to pay this tax. She has also advised you that she accidentally forgot to include quite a substantial trading invoice in her tax return for 2019/20, and is wondering what to do about this and whether she might incur a penalty.

In the box below respond to Mina's query by explaining:

(a) **When she should pay the 2020/21 tax liability** (1 mark)

(b) **How much each payment on account will be for 2021/22 and when these should be paid** (3 marks)

(c) **When the balancing payment 2021/22 would be due and how this is calculated** (3 marks)

(d) The penalty that she may incur for a careless (non deliberate) error on her return, and what she could do to try and reduce this penalty (4 marks)

Task 7 (5 marks)

Crystal is a sole trader who has been trading for many years, has taxable trading profits of £91,750 for the year ended 31 December 2020.

Crystal's Class 2 NIC liability for 2020/21 is: (show your answer to the nearest penny)

£ [   ] . [ ]

Crystal's Class 4 NIC liability for 2020/21 is: (show your answer to the nearest penny)

£ [   ] . [ ]

Pearl is a sole trader who has been trading for many years. She has taxable trading profits of £27,300 for the year ended 31 December 2020.

Pearl's Class 2 NIC liability for 2020/21: (show your answer to the nearest penny)

£ [   ] . [ ]

Pearl's Class 4 NIC liability for 2020/21 is: (show your answer to the nearest penny)

£ [ ] . [ ]

(5 marks)

Task 8 (5 marks)

(a) Identify whether the following statements are true or false.

	True ✓	False ✓
A sole trader must make a claim to set a loss made in 2020/21 against total income in 2020/21before making a claim to set the loss against total income in 2019/20		
A sole trader can carry trade losses forward and choose the best year to use them		
A sole trader can only offset trading losses brought forward against profits of the same trade		

(b) A limited company makes a trading loss of £47,300 in its year ended 31 March 2021. It has also made a chargeable gain of £52,350 in the same period, and has capital losses brought forward of £5,200. The company has a policy of claiming relief for its losses as soon as possible.

(i) The amount of trading loss that can be claimed against profits in the year ended 31 March 2021 is:

£ [ ]

(ii) The amount of trading loss that can be carried forward to the year ended 31 March 2022 is:

£ [ ]

Task 9 (6 marks)

A small or medium sized company incurring qualifying Research and Development costs can obtain extra relief for those costs.

(a) **Briefly define a small or medium sized company, state what those qualifying costs may comprise, and how the extra relief is calculated.** **(4 marks)**

The generous relief for R&D expenditure may lead to tax losses.

(b) **Briefly explain the extra option a company has if the tax loss is created by R&D relief.** **(2 marks)**

Task 10 (9 marks)

(a) **For the following disposals, tick if it would be exempt or chargeable:** **(3 marks)**

	Exempt ✓	Chargeable ✓
Disposal of a vintage car worth £40,000		
Gift of land to a charity		
Gift of jewellery on the taxpayer's death		

(b) Nick bought a five-acre plot of land for £50,000. He sold three acres of the land at auction for £105,000. He had spent £2,500 installing drainage on the three acres which he sold. His disposal costs were £1,500. The market value of the remaining two acres at the date of sale was £45,000.

Calculate the chargeable gain on the disposal of the three acres of land using the table below (do not use brackets or minus signs). **(6 marks)**

	£
Gross proceeds	
Costs of disposal	
Net proceeds	
Cost	
Enhancement expenditure	
Chargeable gain	

Task 11 (14 marks)

In May 2020, Green Ltd sold 4,000 of the shares it held in Blue Ltd for £130,000. These shares had been acquired as follows:

	No. of shares	£
April 1989	2,000	25,000
June 1994	2,000	35,000
July 1997 – bonus issue	1 for 10	
September 2002 – rights issue	1 for 5	£10 per share

Indexation factors:

April 1989 to June 1994	0.266
June 1994 to July 1997	0.088
June 1994 to September 2002	0.227
July 1997 to September 2002	0.128
September 2002 to December 2017	0.620

Calculate the chargeable gain on the sale of these shares in May 2020. **(14 marks)**

BPP PRACTICE ASSESSMENT 1
BUSINESS TAX

ANSWERS

Business Tax (BSTX)
BPP practice assessment 1

Task 1

(a)

	£
Profit for the year per accounts	227,070
Disallowed items added back	
Gifts to customers – cakes	1,350
New wall	2,200
Increase in general provision	400
Private motor expenses – George	1,650
Depreciation charge	21,080
Total to add back	26,680
Allowed items deducted	
Capital allowances	15,000
Adjusted trading profits	238,750

(b)

	Allowed ✓	Disallowed – add back ✓	Disallowed – deduct ✓
Purchase of raw materials	✓		
Private use of vehicle by an employee	✓		
Purchase of delivery van		✓	
Interest received on business bank account			✓

Task 2

(a)

	Jude £	Kelly £	Liam £
Period to:			
30/06/2020			
Division of profits (3:1)	30,375	10,125	0
Period to:			
30/09/2020			
Salary (3 months)	0	0	1,500
Division of profits (2:2:1)	4,800	4,800	2,400
Total profit for y/e 30/09/2020	35,175	14,925	3,900

(b)

(i)   The penultimate tax year is:

2019/20

(ii)   The final tax year is:

2020/21

(iii)   The profits for the penultimate year of trade are:

£ | 45,000

(iv)   The profits for the final year of trade are:

£ | 47,500

Working

(£42,000 + £15,000 – £9,500)

Task 3

	AIA £	Main pool £	Special rate pool £	Owner's car £		Allowances £
Period to 31 December 20						
Additions:						
Plant and machinery	530,400					
Car				16,000		
AIA £1,000,000 × 6/12	(500,000)					500,000
	30,400	30,400				
Disposal		(18,000)				
		12,400				
WDA @ 18% × 6/12				(1,440)	× 75%	1,080
WDA @ 18% × 6/12		(1,116)				1,116
Capital allowances						502,196
Year end 31 December 21		11,284		14,560		
Disposal				(15,300)		
Balancing charge				(740)	× 75%	(555)
Additions:						
Car – salesman			28,000			
Car – Mr Wish				17,500		
WDA @ 6 %			(1,680)			1,680
FYA @ 100%				(17,500)	× 75%	13,125
WDA @ 18%		(2,031)				2,031
Capital allowances						16,281
c/f		9,253	26,320	0		

Task 4

Box 17	£15,000
Box 20	£8,500
Box 21	£7,100
Box 23	£15,600
Box 27	£110
Box 28	£1,500
Box 31	£47,810
Box 35	£2,550
Box 46	£2,550

Task 5

(a)

	✓
One computation from 1 January 2020 to 31 March 2021	
Two computations: one from 1 January 2020 to 31 March 2020 and one from 1 April 2020 to 31 March 2021	
Two computations: one from 1 January 2020 to 31 December 2020 and one from 1 January 2021 to 31 March 2021	✓
It can deal with the computation for whatever period the company chooses	

(b) **(i)** Abbey Ltd's taxable total profits are:

£	688,660

Working

(£620,843 + £67,817)

(ii) The corporation tax payable for the year ended 31 March 2021 is:

£	130,845

Working

	£
£688,660 × 19%	130,845

(iii) The due date for payment is:

01/01/2022

Abbey Ltd is not a large company so pays its corporation tax 9 months and one day after the end of the accounting period.

(c)

	✓
14 October 2020	
14 January 2021	
14 April 2021	✓
1 October 2021	

Task 6

(a) The date by which the tax liability for 2020/21 should be paid is 31 January 2022.

(b) There will be two payments on account for 2021/22. Each will be calculated as 50% of the tax liability for the previous tax year (2020/21). The amount will therefore be £2,112.50 (£4,225 ÷ 2), and will be payable on 31 January during the tax year (31 January 2022) and 31 July after the end of the tax year (31 July 2022).

(c) A balancing payment will be due on 31 January after the end of the tax year (31 January 2023) which will be calculated as the actual amount payable for 2021/22 less the two payments on account.

(d) A penalty may be imposed on Mina as she has been careless and not taken reasonable care when filing her return. The penalty will be 30% of the potential lost revenue (PLR) to HMRC as a result of the error. This may be reduced to 0% if Mina makes an unprompted disclosure of the error, which would be before Mina has reason to believe HMRC might discover the error. Otherwise the penalty could be reduced to 15% of PLR and classed as a prompted disclosure.

Task 7

Crystal's Class 2 NIC liability for 2020/21 is: (show your answer to the nearest penny)

£	158	.	60

Working

(£3.05 × 52)

Crystal's Class 4 NIC liability for 2020/21 is: (show your answer to the nearest penny)

£	4,480	.	00

Working

£(50,000 − 9,500) × 9% + £(91,750 − 50,000) × 2%

= (3,645.00) + (835.00)

Pearl's Class 2 NIC liability for 2020/21 is: (show your answer to the nearest penny)

£	158	.	60

Working

(£3.05 × 52)

Pearl's Class 4 NIC liability for 2020/21 is: (show your answer to the nearest penny)

£	1,602	.	00

Working

£(27,300 − 9,500) × 9%

Task 8

(a)

	True ✓	False ✓
A sole trader must make a claim to set a loss made in 2020/21 against total income in 2020/21 before making a claim to set the loss against total income in 2019/20		✓
A sole trader can carry trade losses forward and choose the best year to use them		✓
A sole trader can only offset trading losses brought forward against profits of the same trade	✓	

A sole trader can make a claim to deduct the loss from total income in the tax year preceding the tax year in which the loss is made whether or not he makes a claim to set it against total income in the tax year of the loss.

A sole trader must offset losses carried forward against the first available profits of the same trade.

(b) **(i)** The amount of trading loss that can be claimed against profits in year ended 31 March 2021 is:

£	47,150

Working

(£52,350 – £5,200)

(ii) The amount of trading loss that can be carried forward to the year ended 31 March 2022 is:

£	150

Task 9

(a)

To be classed as small or medium sized the company must have fewer than 500 employees and have either Turnover of less than 100 million Euros or a Balance Sheet of less than 86 million Euros.

Qualifying research and development costs would include items such as R&D staff costs, consumables, software and utilities.

The relief is 230% of the qualifying revenue expenses.

(b)

The company may surrender its loss in return for an R&D tax credit.

This is calculated as 14.5% of the surrenderable loss, capped at the company's PAYE bill.

Task 10

(a)

	Exempt ✓	Chargeable ✓
Disposal of a vintage car worth £40,000	✓	
Gift of land to a charity	✓	
Gift of jewellery on the taxpayer's death	✓	

(b)

	£
Gross proceeds	105,000
Costs of disposal	1,500
Net proceeds	103,500
Cost (W)	35,000
Enhancement expenditure	2,500
Chargeable gain	66,000

Working Cost $= \dfrac{105,000}{105,000 + 45,000} \times £50,000$ (35,000)

Task 11

	No. of shares	Cost £	Indexed cost £
FA 1985 pool			
April 1989	2,000	25,000	25,000
Index to June 1994 0.266 × £25,000			6,650
Addition	2,000	35,000	35,000
	4,000	60,000	66,650
Bonus issue (N)	400	–	–
	4,400	60,000	66,650
Index to September 2002 0.227 × £66,650			15,130
	4,400	60,000	81,780
Rights issue	880	8,800	8,800
	5,280	68,800	90,580
Index to December 2017 0.620 × £90,580			56,160
	5,280	68,800	146,740
Less sale	(4,000)	(52,121)	(111,167)
	1,280	16,679	35,573
Gain			
Disposal proceeds			130,000
Less cost			(52,121)
Less indexation £(111,167 – 52,121)			(59,046)
Chargeable gain			18,833

Note. There is no need to compute indexation to the date of the bonus issue.

BPP PRACTICE ASSESSMENT 2
BUSINESS TAX

Time allowed: 2 hours

Business Tax (BSTX)
BPP practice assessment 2

In the live assessment you will have access to the Tax tables and reference material which have been reproduced at the back of this Question Bank. Please use them whilst completing this practice assessment so that you are familiar with their content.

....

Task 1 (9 marks)

The statement of profit or loss for Henry Ltd for the year to 31 December 2020 shows the following information:

	£	£
Gross profit		487,500
Profit on sale of shares		12,850
Dividends received		4,500
Property business income		7,500
		512,350
General expenses (note 1)	240,780	
Wages and salaries	120,650	
Administrative expenses	87,230	
Depreciation charge	14,600	
		(463,260)
Profit for the year		49,090

Notes.

1 **General expenses**

These include:

	£
Qualifying charitable donation (paid July 2020)	3,500
Entertaining customers	8,450

2 **Capital allowances**

The capital allowances for the year ended 31 December 2020 are £8,750.

(a) Complete the computation. Do not use minus signs or brackets to show negative figures. Please keep your selected answers in the same order as they appear in the picklist.   (6 marks)

Profit	49,090
Add back (Picklist 1)	
▼	
▼	
▼	
Total added back	
Deduct (Picklist 2)	
▼	
▼	
▼	
▼	
Adjusted trading profits	

Picklist 1:

Qualifying charitable donation (paid July 2020)
Entertaining customers
Wages and salaries
Administrative expenses
Depreciation charge

Picklist 2:

Profit on sale of shares
Dividends received
Property business income
Administrative expenses
Depreciation charge
Capital allowances

(b) For each of the following items, pick the correct treatment in relation to the computation of the taxable profit.   (3 marks)

Capital allowances   ▼

Staff party £10 per head   ▼

Purchase of new motor vehicle   ▼

Picklist:

Allowed
Disallowed and add back
Disallowed and deduct

···

Task 2 (11 marks)

Mustafa has been trading for many years, making up accounts to 31 March.

His capital allowances balances brought forward at 1 April 2020 were as follows:

Main pool	£13,291
Car for Mustafa, 30% private usage	£8,745

The following capital transactions were made in the period:

		£
Additions		
10.04.20	Plant and machinery	58,100
15.04.20	Car for Mustafa, CO_2 emissions 50 g/km, 40% private usage	24,500
22.06.20	Plant and machinery	983,750
Disposal		
15.04.20	Mustafa's previous car	8,000
3.05.20	Plant and machinery (original cost £4,100)	5,970

Using the proforma layout provided, calculate the capital allowances for the year ended 31 March 2021. **(11 marks)**

		AIA £	Main pool £	Private use car (70%) £	Private use car (60%) £	Allowances £

Task 3 (19 marks)

(a) Sayed started trading on 1 January 2020. He makes up his accounts to 30 April each year. The profits were calculated as:

	£
Period to 30 April 2020	20,000
Year to 30 April 2021	36,000
Year to 30 April 2022	42,000

Calculate the taxable profits and state the tax year and basis period for the first three tax years of trading. Insert the tax year dates as XXXX/XX (eg 2015/16) and the basis period dates as XX/XX/XXXX (eg 01/12/2015). **(10 marks)**

	Tax year XXXX/XX	Basis period XX/XX/XXXX – XX/XX/XXXX	Profit £
First year	/	–	
Second year	/	–	
Third year	/	–	

His overlap profits are:

£	

(b) Peter has been in business for several years with a year end of 30 September. In 2021 he decided to change his accounting date to 31 March. His overlap profit on commencement was £3,000 for six months and his recent profits were:

	£
Year ended 30 September 2019	12,000
Year to 30 September 2020	18,000
Period ended 31 March 2021	6,000
Year ended 31 March 2022	24,000

Calculate the taxable profits and state the tax year and basis period for the year of change and the years before and after. Insert the tax year dates as XXXX/XX (eg 2015/16) and the basis period dates as XX/XX/XXXX (eg 30/09/2015). **(9 marks)**

Tax year XXXX/XX	Basis period XX/XX/XXXX – XX/XX/XXXX	Profit £
/	–	
/	–	
/	–	

Task 4 (9 marks)

Aggie Tring has carried on business for many years as a furniture restorer making up accounts to 31 December each year.

The following information is relevant to her period of account to 31 December 2020:

	£
Revenue	144,000
Cost of materials used in restoration	20,000
Travel (20% private)	5,700
Electricity	900
Insurance	360
Office costs	1,800
Bank charges	200
Accountancy	550
Machinery purchased	5,000

Using this information, complete the self employment page.

(9 marks)

Business expenses

Please read the 'Self-employment (full) notes' before filling in this section.

Total expenses	Disallowable expenses
If your annual turnover was below £85,000, you may just put your total expenses in box 31	Use this column if the figures in boxes 17 to 30 include disallowable amounts

17 Cost of goods bought for resale or goods used

£ . 0 0

32

£ . 0 0

18 Construction industry – payments to subcontractors

£ . 0 0

33

£ . 0 0

19 Wages, salaries and other staff costs

£ . 0 0

34

£ . 0 0

20 Car, van and travel expenses

£ . 0 0

35

£ . 0 0

21 Rent, rates, power and insurance costs

£ . 0 0

36

£ . 0 0

22 Repairs and maintenance of property and equipment

£ . 0 0

37

£ . 0 0

23 Phone, fax, stationery and other office costs

£ . 0 0

38

£ . 0 0

24 Advertising and business entertainment costs

£ . 0 0

39

£ . 0 0

25 Interest on bank and other loans

£ . 0 0

40

£ . 0 0

26 Bank, credit card and other financial charges

£ . 0 0

41

£ . 0 0

27 Irrecoverable debts written off

£ . 0 0

42

£ . 0 0

28 Accountancy, legal and other professional fees

£ . 0 0

43

£ . 0 0

29 Depreciation and loss or profit on sale of assets

£ . 0 0

44

£ . 0 0

30 Other business expenses

£ . 0 0

45

£ . 0 0

31 Total expenses (total of boxes 17 to 30)

£ . 0 0

46 Total disallowable expenses (total of boxes 32 to 45)

£ . 0 0

SA103F 2021   Page SEF 2

(Adapted from HMRC, 2020)

Task 5 (10 marks)

A company made up accounts to 31 March 2020. It decides to make up its next set of accounts to 30 September 2021.

(a) **Show how each of the following would be allocated for the long period of account.** **(5 marks)**

	Amount accrued in period ✓	Time apportioned ✓	Period in which it arose ✓
Trading profits			
Business property income			
Qualifying charitable donation			
Chargeable gains			
Non trading interest received			

(b) **Tick the correct box to show whether the following statements are true or false:** **(3 marks)**

	True ✓	False ✓
A company can offset its allowable losses on the disposal of chargeable assets against trading profits.		
A company can carry back its trading losses to set against total profits of the previous 12 months before offsetting losses against current year total profits.		
The carry forward of a company's trading loss is an 'all or nothing' claim.		

A company has the following information for the year ended 31 December 2020:

- Taxable total profits are £495,000.
- Dividends received are £10,800.
- The company has two related 51% group companies.

(c) **What is the first date by which the company has to pay some or all of its corporation tax liability? (XX/XX/XXXX) (2 marks)**

Task 6 (4 marks)

Polly is a sole trader who has taxable trading profits of £66,650 in 2020/21.

The amount chargeable to national insurance Class 4 contributions at 9% is:

£ [   ]

The amount chargeable to national insurance Class 4 contributions at 2% is:

£ [   ]

The total amount of national insurance payable by Polly in 2020/21 is:

£ [   ] . [   ]

Task 7 (7 marks)

(a) (i) **The maximum penalty for failure to keep records for each tax year or accounting period is:**

	✓
£4,000	
£3,000	
£2,500	
£1,500	

(ii) **The maximum penalty for a deliberate but not concealed error as a percentage of Potential Lost Revenue is:**

	✓
70%	
35%	
20%	
15%	

(iii) A taxpayer files his tax return for 2020/21 online on 15 March 2022. His tax liability for the year is £2,000.

The maximum penalty for late filing is:

	✓
£2,000	
£300	
£200	
£100	

(3 marks)

(b) Holly has a liability to capital gains tax in 2020/21.

(i) **She must pay the capital gains tax due by: (insert dates as xx/xx/xxxx)**

Holly is also required to make payments on account for her 2020/21 income tax liability.

(ii) **She must make payments on account for 2020/21 by:**

and

(iii) **She must pay the balancing payment by:**

(4 marks)

Task 8 (5 marks)

JDP, a sole trader who has been trading for many years, made a trading profit of £4,500 in his year ended 31 January 2020, a trading loss of £45,000 in his year ended 31 January 2021, and he predicts trading profits to be £5,000 for the year ended 31 January 2022. Each tax year he also receives rental income of £9,000, and in December 2020 he sold a painting and made a chargeable gain of £17,000.

JDP has a policy of claiming the maximum amount of loss relief as early as possible, in all possible ways.

How much trading loss will JDP relieve against net income in 2019/20?

£ [   ]

How much trading loss will JDP relieve against net income in 2020/21?

£ [   ]

How much trading loss will JDP relieve against his chargeable gain in 2020/21?

£ [   ]

Tick the correct box to show whether the following statement is true or false:

	True ✓	False ✓
In 2020/21 JDP could choose to just set the loss against the capital gain, so as not to lose the benefit of his personal allowance		

What is the maximum trading loss JDP can relieve in 2021/22?

£ [   ]

....

Task 9 (6 marks)

(a) Fill in the blanks using the picklist below: **(2 marks)**

An employed person usually has a contract _____ service, where as a self-employed person will have a contract _____ services.

Picklist:

for
of

(b) **Fred is doing some work for Howard Limited. Tick the relevant column to show whether the following factors would tend to imply that Fred is employed or self-employed:** **(4 marks)**

	Employed ✓	Self-employed ✓
Fred has permission to work for several clients		
Howard Ltd pay Fred sick and holiday pay		
Howard Ltd provide all the equipment which Fred needs		
Fred has control over when and where he performs the work		

Task 10 (10 marks)

Purple Ltd had the following transactions in the shares of Yellow Ltd:

May 1989	Purchased 4,000 shares for £8,000
May 2003	Took up one for two rights issue at £3 per share
October 2020	Sold all the shares for £32,000

Assumed Indexation factors

May 1989 to May 2003	0.578
May 2003 to December 2017	0.532

Using the proforma layout provided, calculate the chargeable gain arising from the sale of the shares in Yellow Ltd.

Share pool

	No. of shares	Cost £	Indexed cost £

Gain

	£

....

Task 11 (10 marks)

Georgia sold her business which she had run for twenty years to Milly on 10 October 2020. The only chargeable asset was her shop which Georgia had bought in February 2009 for £82,500. She spent £17,000 on building an extension in June 2011. The sale proceeds relating to the shop were £225,000. Georgia claimed business asset disposal relief on the disposal.

(a) **Using the proforma layout provided, calculate Georgia's capital gains tax liability for 2020/21. She had made no other chargeable gains during the year.** **(6 marks)**

	£
Sale proceeds	
Cost	
Enhancement expenditure	
Net gain	
Annual exempt amount	
Taxable gain	
CGT payable	

On 1 November 2020 Mike sold a factory used in his business for £600,000. The factory had cost £175,000. Mike had purchased a replacement factory for £750,000 on 1 September 2020.

(b) How much of Mike's capital gain on the disposal of the original factory can be deferred by a rollover relief claim?

(2 marks)

	✓
£150,000	
£575,000	
£175,000	
£425,000	

(c) If Mike's replacement factory had instead cost him £500,000, the amount of the gain that would be chargeable to CGT in 2020/21 is: (2 marks)

£ _____

....

BPP PRACTICE ASSESSMENT 2
BUSINESS TAX

ANSWERS

Business Tax (BSTX)
BPP practice assessment 2

Task 1

(a)

Profit	49,090
Add back	
Qualifying charitable donation (paid July 2020)	3,500
Entertaining customers	8,450
Depreciation charge	14,600
Total added back	26,550
Deduct	
Profit on sale of shares	12,850
Dividends received	4,500
Property business income	7,500
Capital allowances	8,750
Adjusted trading profits	42,040

(b)

Capital allowances	Allowed
Staff party £10 per head	Allowed
Purchase of new motor vehicle	Disallowed and add back

Task 2

Year ended 31 March 2021

	AIA £	Main pool £	Private use car (70%) £	Private use car (60%) £	Allowances £
b/f		13,291	8,745		
AIA additions					
April 2020	58,100				
June 2020	983,750				
Car April 2020				24,500	
AIA	(800,000)				800,000
Transfer to pool	(241,850)	241,850			
Disposals		(4,100)	(8,000)		
		251,041			
BA			745 × 70%		522
WDA @ 18%		(45,187)			45,187
FYA @ 100%				(24,500) × 60%	14,700
c/f		205,854		0	
Total allowances					860,409

Note. The AIA limit fell from £1,000,000 to £200,000 on 1 January 2021. The revised limit for the period is (1,000,000 × 9/12) + (200,000 × 3/12)= 800,000

Task 3

(a)

	Tax year XXXX/XX	Basis period XX/XX/XXXX – XX/XX/XXXX	Profit £
First year	2019/20	01/01/2020 – 05/04/2020	15,000
Second year	2020/21	01/01/2020 – 31/12/2020	44,000
Third year	2021/22	01/05/2020 – 30/04/2021	36,000

Working

Second year: Period ending 30 April 2020 plus 8 months to 31 December 2020

£20,000 + (8/12 × £36,000) = £44,000

His overlap profits are:

£	39,000

Working

Overlap period: 1 January 2020 to 5 April 2020 and 1 May 2020 to 31 December 2020-

Overlap profits: 3/4 × £20,000 + 8/12 × £36,000

(b)

Tax year XXXX/XX	Basis period XX/XX/XXXX – XX/XX/XXXX	Profit £
2019/20	01/10/2018 – 30/09/2019	12,000
2020/21	01/10/2019 – 31/03/2021	21,000
2021/22	01/04/2021 – 31/03/2022	24,000

Working

The year of change is 2020/21

For 2019/20 and 2021/22 the profits are allocated on a current year basis.

For 2020/21 there are two periods ending in the tax year. In this case, we tax them both and relieve overlap:

Year ended 30 September 2020 (12 months)	18,000
Period ended 31 March 2021 (6 months)	6,000
Relieve overlap to bring profits down to 12 months	(3,000)
Taxable profits 2020/21	21,000

Task 4

Box 17	£20,000
Box 20	£5,700
Box 21	£1,260
Box 23	£1,800
Box 26	£200
Box 28	£550
Box 31	£29,510
Box 35	£1,140
Box 46	£1,140

....

Task 5

(a)

	Amount accrued in period ✓	Time apportioned ✓	Period in which it arose ✓
Trading profits		✓	
Business property income		✓	
Qualifying charitable donation			✓
Chargeable gains			✓
Non trading interest received	✓		

(b)

	True ✓	False ✓
A company can offset its allowable losses on the disposal of chargeable assets against trading profits.		✓
A company can carry back its trading losses to set against total profits of the previous 12 months before offsetting losses against current year total profits.		✓
The carry forward of a company's trading loss is an 'all or nothing' claim		✓

A company can offset its allowable losses on the disposal of chargeable assets only against chargeable gains.

A company must offset trading losses in the current period first, whereas an individual trader can offset trading losses in the current and prior year in any order.

A company may choose how much of its loss to use up in the carry forward claim so as not to waste qualifying donations.

(c)

14/07/2020

Working

Annual profit limit = £1,500,000/3 = £500,000 (share with 2 other related companies)

Augmented profits = £495,000 + £10,800 = £505,800

Hence the company is large for corporation tax payment purposes.

Task 6

The amount chargeable to national insurance Class 4 contributions at 9% is:

£	40,500

Working

£(50,000 – 9,500)

The amount chargeable to national insurance Class 4 contributions at 2% is:

£	16,650

Working

£(66,650 – 50,000)

The total amount of national insurance payable by Polly for 2020/21 is:

£	4,136	.	60

Working

Class 2 = £3.05 × 52 weeks = £158.60
Class 4 = £40,500 × 9% + £16,650 × 2% = £3,978.00

Total NIC: £(158.60 + 3978.00) = £4,136.60

....

Task 7

(a) (i)

	✓
£4,000	
£3,000	✓
£2,500	
£1,500	

(ii)

	✓
70%	✓
35%	
20%	
15%	

(iii)

	✓
£2,000	
£300	
£200	
£100	✓

Initial penalty for filing return late is £100. As it is less than 3 months late no further penalty is payable.

(b) (i) She must pay the capital gains tax due by:

31/01/2022

(ii) She must make payments on account for 2020/21 by:

31/01/2021

and

31/07/2021

(iii) She must pay the balancing payment by:

31/01/2022

Task 8

The trading loss which JDP will relieve against net income in 2019/20 is:

£	13,500

(£4,500 + £9,000) The loss cannot be restricted to save the personal allowance

The trading loss which JDP will relieve against net income in 2020/21 is:

£	9,000

The loss cannot be restricted to save the personal allowance

The amount of trading loss which JDP will relieve against his chargeable gain of 2020/21 is:

£	17,000

The loss cannot be restricted to save the annual exempt amount (only capital losses brought forward can be restricted in this way, as they are offset after the annual exempt amount).

	True ✓	False ✓
In 2020/21 JDP could choose to just set the loss against the capital gain, so as not to lose the benefit of his personal allowance		✓

In order to use the trading loss against the gain, JDP must offset the loss against net income first, despite the fact that it would have been covered by his personal allowance.

The maximum trading loss JDP can relieve in 2021/22 is:

£	5,000

Losses can only be offset against trading profits when carried forward.

....

Task 9

(a) An employed person usually has a contract ⬚ of ⬚ service, whereas a self-employed person will have a contract ⬚ for ⬚ services.

(b)

	Employed ✓	Self-employed ✓
Fred has permission to work for several clients		✓
Howard Ltd pay Fred sick and holiday pay	✓	
Howard Ltd provide all the equipment which Fred needs	✓	
Fred has control over when and where he performs the work		✓

....

Task 10

Share pool

	No. of shares	Cost £	Indexed cost £
May 1989	4,000	8,000	8,000
Indexed rise to May 2003			
£8,000 × 0.578			4,624
			12,624
Rights issue 1:2 @ £3	2,000	6,000	6,000
	6,000	14,000	18,624
Indexed rise to December 2017			
£18,624 × 0.532			9,908
	6,000	14,000	28,532

Gain

	£
Disposal proceeds	32,000
Less cost	(14,000)
	18,000
Less indexation (£28,532 – £14,000)	(14,532)
Chargeable gain	3,468

Task 11

(a)

	£
Sale proceeds	225,000
Cost	(82,500)
Enhancement expenditure	(17,000)
Net gain	125,500
Annual exempt amount	(12,300)
Taxable gain	113,200
CGT payable @ 10%	11,320

(b)

	✓
£150,000	
£575,000	
£175,000	
£425,000	✓

Working

	£
Proceeds	600,000
Less cost	(175,000)
Chargeable gain	425,000

Mike reinvested all of the proceeds in a replacement business asset in the period 12 months before/3 years after the disposal so the whole gain of £425,000 can be rolled-over.

(c) | £ | 100,000 |

This is the amount of proceeds that have not been reinvested.

BPP PRACTICE ASSESSMENT 3 BUSINESS TAX

Time allowed: 2 hours

PRACTICE ASSESSMENT 3

Business Tax (BSTX)
BPP practice assessment 3

In the live assessment you will have access to the Tax tables and reference material which have been reproduced at the back of this Question Bank. Please use them whilst completing this practice assessment so that you are familiar with their content.

··

Task 1 (10 marks)

You have been given the following information about Robbie Ltd that relates to the year ended 31 March 2021:

	£	£
Gross profit		801,220
Profit on sale of shares		45,777
Dividends received		40,500
		887,497
General expenses (note 1)	455,100	
Administrative expenses	122,010	
Wages and salaries	137,567	(714,677)
Profit for the year		172,820

Note.

1   General expenses:

These include:

	£
Qualifying charitable donation	5,000
Parking fines paid for a director	160
Depreciation charge	65,230
Subscription to a trade association	1,000
Donation to a political party	850

Note.

2   Capital allowances:

     These have already been calculated at £38,750.

(a)   Complete the computation. Do not use minus signs or brackets to show negative figures. Please keep your selected answers in the same order as they appear in the picklist.   (7 marks)

Profit		172,820
Disallowed items added back (Picklist 1)		
	▼	
	▼	
	▼	
	▼	
Total added back		
Allowed items deducted (Picklist 2)		
	▼	
	▼	
	▼	
Total deducted		
Adjusted trading profits		

Picklist 1:

Qualifying charitable donation
Parking fines paid for a director
Depreciation charge
Subscription to a trade association
Donation to a political party
Administrative expenses
Wages and salaries

Picklist 2:

Profit on sale of shares
Dividends received
Administrative expenses
Wages and salaries
Capital allowances

(b) **Identify whether the following statements are true or false.**

(3 marks)

	True ✓	False ✓
Badges of trade have developed mainly through case law.		
If a trader inherits an asset and he sells it shortly afterwards, it will appear likely that he is trading.		
If a trader enhances an asset to make it more desirable to a buyer, this is indicative of trading.		

Task 2 (10 marks)

Gerry and Harold have been in partnership for many years making up accounts to 31 December each year sharing profits 2:1 respectively.

On 1 January 2021, Iris joined the partnership. Profits are then shared 2:2:1 for Gerry, Harold and Iris.

For the year ended 31 December 2020, the partnership trading profit was £27,000 and for the year ended 31 December 2021 was £35,000.

(a) **Using the proforma layout provided, show the division of profit between the partners for the year ended 31 December 2020 and 31 December 2021. Fill in all boxes and add a 0 (zero) if necessary.** **(6 marks)**

	Total £	Gerry £	Harold £	Iris £
Year ended 31.12.20				
Year ended 31.12.21				

(b) **The taxable trading profit for each partner for 2020/21 is:**

(4 marks)

Gerry:

£ [   ]

Harold:

£ [   ]

Iris:

£ [   ]

Task 3 (12 marks)

Ian Goodwin commenced trading on 1 October 2020, and made his first accounts up to 31 December 2021. Ian Goodwin's capital transactions from the date of commencement are:

Additions:		£
10 October 2020	Plant and machinery	550,000
1 May 2021	Motor van	35,500
1 November 2021	Car, 30% private usage by Ian (CO$_2$ emissions 152g/km)	9,600
15 December 2021	Car, 20% private usage by an employee (CO$_2$ emissions 48g/km)	12,500

Calculate the capital allowances for the 15-month period ended 31 December 21.

Task 4 (11 marks)

You act for Freshly Fish, a partnership of fishmongers. The partners are Fred Fisher and his son George. The partnership profits are divided 2:1 between Fred and George. The partnership makes up accounts to 31 March each year.

The following information relates to the year to 31 March 2021:

	£
Revenue	210,000
Cost of fish sold	70,000
Allowable expenses	69,710
Capital allowances	13,200

Use this information to complete page 6 of the partnership tax return for Fred Fisher.

Partnership Statement (short) for the year ended 5 April 2021

Please read these instructions before completing the Statement

Use these pages to allocate partnership income if the only income for the relevant
return period was trading and professional income or untaxed interest and alternative
finance receipts from UK banks and building societies. Otherwise you must download the
'Partnership Statement (Full)' pages to record details of the allocation of all the partnership
income. Go to www.gov.uk/taxreturnforms

Step 1   Fill in boxes 1 to 29 and boxes A and B as appropriate. Get the figures you need
from the relevant boxes in the Partnership Tax Return. Complete a separate
Statement for each accounting period covered by this Partnership Tax Return and
for each trade or profession carried on by the partnership.

Step 2   Then allocate the amounts in boxes 11 to 29 attributable to each partner using the
allocation columns on this page and page 7, read the Partnership Tax Return
Guide, go to www.gov.uk/taxreturnforms
If the partnership has more than 3 partners, please photocopy page 7.

Step 3   Each partner will need a copy of their allocation of income to fill in their personal
tax return.

PARTNERSHIP INFORMATION
If the partnership business includes a trade or
profession, enter here the accounting period for
which appropriate items in this statement
are returned.

Start **1** / /

End **2** / /

Nature of trade **3**

MIXED PARTNERSHIPS

Tick here if this Statement is drawn
up using Corporation Tax rules **4**

Tick here if this Statement is drawn up
using tax rules for non-residents **5**

Individual partner details

6 Name of partner

Address

Postcode

Date appointed as a partner
(if during 2019-20 or 2020-21) Partner's Unique Taxpayer Reference (UTR)

7 / /   **8**

Date ceased to be a partner
(if during 2019-20 or 2020-21) Partner's National Insurance number

9 / /   **10**

Partnership's profits, losses, income and tax credits

Tick this box if the items
entered in the box had
foreign tax taken off ▼

Partner's share of profits, losses, income and tax credits

Copy figures in boxes 11 to 29 to boxes in the individual's
Partnership (short) pages as shown below

- for an accounting period ended in 2020/21 ▼

from box 3.83	Profit from a trade or profession **A**	**11** £	Profit **11** £ — Copy this figure to box 8
from box 3.82	Adjustment on change of basis	**11A** £	**11A** £ — Copy this figure to box 10
from box 3.84	Loss from a trade or profession **B**	**12** £	Loss **12** £ — Copy this figure to box 8
from box 3.94	Disguised remuneration	**12A**	**12A** — Copy to box 15

- for the period 6 April 2020 to 5 April 2021*

from box 7.9A	Income from untaxed UK savings	**13** £	**13** £ — Copy this figure to box 28
from box 3.97	CIS deductions made by contractors on account of tax	**24** £	**24** £ — Copy this figure to box 30
from box 3.98	Other tax taken off trading income	**24A** £	**24A** £ — Copy this figure to box 31
from box 3.117	Partnership charges	**29** £	**29** £ — Copy this figure to box 4, 'Other tax reliefs' section on page Ai 2 in your personal tax return

* If you're a 'CT Partnership' see the Partnership Tax Return Guide

SA800 2021   PARTNERSHIP TAX RETURN: PAGE 6

(Adapted from HMRC, 2020)

Task 5 (4 marks)

Z plc makes up accounts for a 15 month period to 31 March 2021.

(a) **Identify how the company will apportion its property income for the long period of account between the accounting periods. Tick ONE box.** **(1 mark)**

	✓
Any way the company chooses	
On a time basis	
On an accruals basis	
On a receipts basis	

(b) **Decide how the company will deal with its capital allowances computations for the long period of account. Tick ONE box.** **(1 mark)**

	✓
One computation for the whole 15 month period prorating the allowances up accordingly	
Two computations; one for 12 months, and one for 3 months prorating the allowances down accordingly	

A company has the following information for the 9 months to 30 June 2020:

- Trading profits are £90,900.
- Dividends received are £13,500.
- The company has no related 51% group companies.

(c) **The corporation tax liability for nine months to 30 June 2020 is:** **(2 marks)**

£ [   ]

....

Task 6 (2 marks)

Jayden starts in business as a sole trader on 6 April 2020. Her adjusted trading profit for the year to 5 April 2021 is £22,500.

(a) **Jayden's Class 2 NICs payable for 2020/21 are:**

£ [   ] . [   ]

(b) **Jayden's Class 4 NICs payable for 2020/21 are:**

£ [   ] . [   ]

....

Task 7 (5 marks)

You have been instructed by a new client who started trading on 1 May 2020. He is concerned about some important dates when he should contact HM Revenue & Customs. He has never filled in a tax return.

State:

(a) **The date when he should inform HM Revenue & Customs that he is chargeable to income tax: (insert dates as xx/xx/xxxx)**

(1 mark)

```
┌──────────────┐
│              │
└──────────────┘
```

(b) **The date when his first tax return should be filed, if it is to be filed online:** **(1 mark)**

```
┌──────────────┐
│              │
└──────────────┘
```

(c) **The date income tax will have to be paid (assuming he has any) for his first year of trading:** **(1 mark)**

```
┌──────────────┐
│              │
└──────────────┘
```

(d) **The date until which he must keep his business records in relation to his first tax year as a trader:** **(1 mark)**

```
┌──────────────┐
│              │
└──────────────┘
```

(e) **The date of his first payment on account in respect of his income tax and Class 4 national insurance for his second tax year as a trader:** **(1 mark)**

```
┌──────────────┐
│              │
└──────────────┘
```

Task 8 (12 marks)

(a) Zowie Ltd, a trading company, made a trading loss of £100,000 in its year ended 31 March 2021. It has trading income of £500,000 and other income of £250,000 in each of the years ending 31 March 2020, 2021 and 2022.

Identify whether the following statements are true or false.
(4 marks)

	True ✓	False ✓
Zowie Ltd can set its loss against its total income in the year ended 31 March 2021.		
Zowie Ltd can carry its loss forward against its trading profits in the year ended 31 March 2022.		
Zowie Ltd can set its loss against its total income in the year ended 31 March 2022.		
Zowie Ltd can set its loss against its total income in in the year ended 31 March 2020.		

(b) Donna has traded for many years, making up accounts to 30 June each year. Her recent results have been:

Year ended	£
30 June 2018	32,000
30 June 2019	(66,000)
30 June 2020	18,000

She has received property income as follows:

	£
2018/19	6,000
2019/20	16,000
2020/21	21,000

Using the proforma layout provided, compute Donna's net income for 2018/19 to 2020/21, assuming maximum claims for loss relief are made as early as possible. If an answer is zero, insert 0, and show the offset of losses within brackets. Fill in all boxes. **(7 marks)**

	2018/19 £	2019/20 £	2020/21 £
Trading profits			
Trading loss offset against future year			
Property income			
Trading loss offset against current year			
Trading loss offset against previous year			
Net income			

(c)   The amount of Donna's loss which will be carried forward to 2021/22 will be: **(1 mark)**

£ [   ]

Task 9 (6 marks)

You receive the following email from a client.

From: Charlotte@berkshire.com
To: accountant@advice.com

I am thinking of setting up a limited company and offering my services as a PR consultant through my company.

I am currently employed as a PR Manager but think I may be better off if I work through a company and invoice my employer, as a friend has told me I would pay less tax that way.

I would be grateful if you would send me some more information.

Many thanks

Charlotte

(a)   Briefly summarise the IR35 legislation.   (3 marks)

(b)   Explain whether or not you think the IR35 legislation may affect Charlotte.   (3 marks)

Task 10 (13 marks)

Treasure Ltd sold 2,500 shares in Williams Ltd for £102,100 in June 2020.

2,000 shares had been bought in November 2001 for £50,000.

In February 2006, Treasure Ltd took up a rights issue of 1 for 2 shares, at £20 per share.

Indexation factors

November 2001 to February 2006   0.119
February 2006 to December 2017   0.432

Using the proforma layout provided, calculate the capital gain arising from the disposal of the shares in Williams Ltd. Clearly show the number of shares, and their value, to carry forward.

(13 marks)

Share pool

	No. of shares	Cost £	Indexed cost £

Gain

	£

Task 11 (15 marks)

(a) DEF plc bought a factory for use in its trade on 10 December 2010 for £120,000. It sold the factory for £230,000 on 1 May 2020. **(4 marks)**

Assumed Indexation factors

December 2010 to December 2017   0.218

(i) **The gain on disposal of the factory is:**

£ [ ]

(ii) **The dates during which a new asset must be acquired for a rollover relief claim to be made are between: (insert dates as xx/xx/xxxx)**

[ ]

and

[ ]

(iii) **If a new factory is acquired for £200,000, the amount of the gain which can be rolled-over is:**

£ [ ]

(b) Sami gives a shop which he has used in his trade to his son Troy in August 2020. The shop was acquired for £120,000 and was worth £150,000 at the date of the gift. A claim for gift relief is made.

Identify which of the following statements are correct, by ticking one or more statements. (3 marks)

	✓
Troy will acquire the shop with a base cost of £120,000.	
Sami will have no chargeable gain on the gift.	
The annual exempt amount is deducted before gift relief.	
Troy will acquire the shop with a base cost of £150,000.	

(c) Dani made two capital disposals in 2020/21:

1. the disposal of her trade on 1 November 2020, making total chargeable gains of £120,000

2. the disposal of an investment building on 13 February 2021, making a chargeable gain of £70,000

Dani had taxable income (after the deduction of her personal allowance) of £25,500 in 2020/21. She also has a capital loss of £36,000 brought forward from 2019/20.

(i) The taxable gain subject to capital gains tax at 10% is:

£ [ ]

(ii) The taxable gain subject to capital gains tax at 20% is:

£ [ ]

(iii) Dani's capital gains tax liability in 2020/21 is:

£ [ ]

(iv) The date by which the capital gains tax must be paid (xx/xx/xxx):

[ ]

(8 marks)

BPP PRACTICE ASSESSMENT 3
BUSINESS TAX

ANSWERS

Business Tax (BSTX)
BPP practice assessment 3

Task 1

(a)

Profit	172,820
Disallowed items added back	
Qualifying charitable donation	5,000
Parking fines paid for a director	160
Depreciation charge	65,230
Donation to a political party	850
Total added back	71,240
Allowed items deducted	
Profit on sale of shares	45,777
Dividends received	40,500
Capital allowances	38,750
Total deducted	125,027
Adjusted trading profits	119,033

(b)

	True ✓	False ✓
Badges of trade have developed mainly through case law.	✓	
If a trader inherits an asset and he sells it shortly afterwards, it will appear likely that he is trading.		✓
If a trader enhances an asset to make it more desirable to a buyer, this is indicative of trading.	✓	

Task 2

(a)

	Total £	Gerry £	Harold £	Iris £
Year ended 31.12.20	27,000	18,000	9,000	0
Year ended 31.12.21	35,000	14,000	14,000	7,000

(b) The taxable trading profit for each partner for 2020/21 is:

Gerry:

£	18,000

Harold:

£	9,000

Iris:

£	1,750

Working

Gerry and Harold

y/e 31.12.20 current year basis

Iris

First year of trading: actual basis 1 January 2021 to 5 April 2021

$3/12 \times £7,000$

Task 3

	AIA £	FYA £	Main pool £	Car (70%) £	Allowances £
AIA additions					
Plant and machinery	550,000				
Motor van	35,500				
	585,500				
AIA (see note)	(450,000)				450,000
	135,500				
Transfer balance to main pool	(135,500)		135,500		
Non-AIA additions					
Car				9,600	
Car		12,500			
FYA @ 100%		(12,500)			12,500
WDA @ 18% × 15/12			(30,488)		30,488
WDA @ 6% × 15/12				(720) × 70%	504
c/f			105,012	8,880	
Allowances					493,492

Note. The WDA is time apportioned for a long period of account, but not the FYA.

The AIA limit fell from £1,000,000 to £200,000 on 1 January 2021. The maximum for the period is (3/12 x £1,000,000) + (12/12 x £200,000) = £450,000

Task 4

Partnership tax adjusted trading profit £(210,000 − 70,000 − 69,710 − 13,200) = £57,090

Page 6

Box 1	01.04.20
Box 2	31.03.21
Box 3	Fishmongers
Box 11	£57,090
Box 6	Fred Fisher
Box 11	£38,060

....

Task 5

(a)

	✓
Any way the company chooses	
On a time basis	✓
On an accruals basis	
On a receipts basis	

(b)

	✓
One computation for the whole 15 month period prorating the allowances up accordingly	
Two computations; one for 12 months, and one for 3 months prorating the allowances down accordingly	✓

(c) The corporation tax liability for nine months to 30 June 2020 is:

£	17,271

Working

Dividends are not taxable so TTP = £90,900

£90,900 × 19% = £17,271

....

Task 6

(a) Jayden's Class 2 NICs payable for 2020/21 are:

£	158	.	60

Working

(£3.05 × 52)

(b) Jayden's Class 4 NICs payable for 2020/21 are:

£	1,170	.	00

Working

(22,500 – 9,500) × 9%.

Task 7

(a) The date when he should inform HM Revenue & Customs that he is chargeable to income tax:

05/10/2021

(b) The date when his first tax return should be filed, if it is to be filed online:

31/01/2022

(c) The date income tax will need to be paid (assuming he has any) for his first year of trading:

31/01/2022

(d) **The date until which he must keep his business records in relation to his first tax year as a trader:**

31/01/2027

(e) **The date of his first payment on account in respect of his income tax and Class 4 national insurance for his second tax year as a trader:**

31/01/2022

Task 8

(a)

	True ✓	False ✓
Zowie Ltd can set its loss against its total income in the year ended 31 March 2021.	✓	
Zowie Ltd can carry its loss forward against its trading profits in the year ended 31 March 2022.		✓
Zowie Ltd can set its loss against its total income in the year ended 31 March 2022.	✓	
Zowie Ltd can set its loss against its total income in in the year ended 31 March 2020.		✓

(b)

	2018/19 £	2019/20 £	2020/21 £
Trading profits	32,000	0	18,000
Trading loss offset against future year			(12,000)
Property income	6,000	16,000	21,000
Trading loss offset against current year		(16,000)	
Trading loss offset against previous year	(38,000)		
Net income	0	0	27,000

(c) **The amount of Donna's loss which will be carried forward to 2021/22 will be:**

£	0

Task 9

(a)

> The IR35 legislation exists to prevent Personal Service Companies (PSCs) being used to disguise employment.
>
> It is applied where the relationship between the client and the worker would be deemed to be one of employment, were it not for the existence of the PSC.
>
> The effect of the legislation is for the client's payments to be taxed as employment income on the worker.

(b)

> If Charlotte carries on doing the same job for the same company then HMRC are likely to consider her to have an employment relationship, and the legislation would apply to her.

Task 10

Share pool

	No. of shares	Cost £	Indexed cost £
November 2001	2,000	50,000	50,000
Index to February 2006			
£50,000 × 0.119			5,950
Rights issue 1 for 2 @ £20 each	1,000	20,000	20,000
	3,000	70,000	75,950
Index to December 2017			
£75,950 × 0.432			32,810
	3,000	70,000	108,760
Less sale	(2,500)	(58,333)	(90,633)
Carry forward	500	11,667	18,127

Gain

			£
Disposal proceeds			102,100
Less cost			(58,333)
			43,767
Indexation (90,633 – 58,333)			(32,300)
Chargeable gain			11,467

Task 11

(a) **(i)** The gain on disposal of the factory is:

£	83,840

Workings

	£
Proceeds of sale	230,000
Less cost	(120,000)
	110,000
Less indexation allowance £120,000 × 0.218	(26,160)
Chargeable gain	83,840

(ii) The dates during which a new asset must be acquired for a rollover relief claim to be made are between:

01/05/2019

and

01/05/2023

(iii) If a new factory is acquired for £200,000, the amount of the gain which can be rolled-over is:

£	53,840

Workings

Gain immediately chargeable £(230,000 – 200,000) = £30,000
Gain which can be rolled-over £(83,840 – 30,000) = £53,840

(b)

	✓
Troy will acquire the shop with a base cost of £120,000.	✓
Sami will have no chargeable gain on the gift.	✓
The annual exempt amount is deducted before gift relief.	
Troy will acquire the shop with a base cost of £150,000.	

Troy will acquire the shop at MV less gift relief £(150,000 – 30,000), gift relief of £30,000 leaves Sami with no gain.

Gift relief cannot be restricted to allow Sami to use his annual exempt amount.

(c) **(i)** The taxable gain subject to capital gains tax at 10% is:

£	120,000

(ii) The taxable gain subject to capital gains tax at 20% is:

£	21,700

(iii) Dani's capital gains tax liability in 2020/21 is:

£	16,340

(iv) The date by which the capital gains tax must be paid (xx/xx/xxx):

31/01/2022

	BADR gains £	Other gains £	
Disposal of trade	120,000	70,000	
Annual exempt amount		(12,300)	
Loss brought forward		(36,000)	
Taxable gains	120,000	21,700	
	10%	20%	
CGT liability	12,000	4,340	16,340

BPP PRACTICE ASSESSMENT 4
BUSINESS TAX

Time allowed: 2 hours

Business Tax (BSTX)
BPP practice assessment 4

In the live assessment you will have access to the Tax tables and reference material which have been reproduced at the back of this Question Bank. Please use them whilst completing this practice assessment so that you are familiar with their content.

Task 1

The statement of profit or loss Jeremy Ltd for the year to 31 March 2021 shows the following information:

	£	£
Gross profit		512,500
Profit on sale of shares		13,550
Dividends received		6,300
Interest income		4,500
		536,850
General expenses (note 1)	210,780	
Motor expenses (note 2)	40,500	
Wages and salaries	110,350	
Administrative expenses	77,230	
Depreciation charge	15,700	
		(454,560)
Profit for the year		82,290

Notes.

1 **General expenses**

These include:

	£
Qualifying charitable donation (paid August 2020)	500
Entertaining customers	9,550
Entertaining staff	8,650

2 **Motor expenses**

These include:

	£
Parking fines incurred by director	610
Petrol used by director for private use	6,300
Leasing costs of car for director (CO_2 emissions 160 g/km)	9,300

3 **Capital allowances**

The capital allowances for the year ended 31 March 2021 are £8,750.

Using the proforma layout provided, compute the adjusted trading profit for Jeremy Ltd for the year to 31 March 2021. Fill in all unshaded boxes. Add a 0 (zero) if necessary.

	£	£
Profit for the year per accounts		82,290
	Add	Deduct
Profit on sale of shares		
Dividends received		
Interest income		
Qualifying charitable donation		
Entertaining customers		
Entertaining staff		
Parking fines incurred by director		
Petrol used by director for private use		

	£	£
Leasing costs of car for director		
Wages and salaries		
Administrative expenses		
Depreciation charge		
Capital allowances		
Total to add/deduct		
Taxable trading profit		

Task 2

Xavier, Yvonne and Zebedee have been in partnership for many years making up accounts to 30 September each year. Under the partnership agreement, Xavier was entitled to a salary of £9,000 a year and the profits were then divided 2:2:1 between the partners respectively.

Xavier retired from the partnership on 31 December 2020. Yvonne and Zebedee carried on the partnership and the partnership agreement was altered so that the profits were then divided 2:1 between Yvonne and Zebedee respectively.

The partnership profits for the year to 30 September 2021 were £209,000.

(a) **Using the proforma layout provided, show the division of the partnership profit for the year to 30 September 2021. Fill in all unshaded boxes and add a 0 (zero) if necessary.**

	Total £	Xavier £	Yvonne £	Zebedee £
Period to 31/12/2020				
Salary				
Share of profits				
Period to 30/09/2021				
Share of profits				
Total profit for y/e 30/09/2021				

You see from your files that Xavier's share of the partnership profit for the year to 30 September 2020 was £21,000 and that he had overlap profits of £4,500 on commencement.

(b) **Xavier's taxable partnership profits for the tax year of cessation are:**

£ [   ]

....

Task 3

Codie is in business as a sole trader making up accounts to 31 January each year. You have been asked to complete her capital allowances computation for the year to 31 January 2021. The following information is relevant:

(1) The capital allowance computation showed the following written-down value at 1 February 2020:

	£
Main pool	58,060

(2) During the period 1 February 2020 to 31 January 2021 Codie had the following capital transactions:

Purchases		£
June 2020	Plant and machinery	900,000
December 2020	Plant and machinery	204,250
January 2021	Car (CO_2 emissions 90g/km)	19,320 (80% private use)
Disposals		
January 2021	Plant and machinery	23,900

Compute Codie's capital allowances for the year to 31 January 2021.

Task 4

You act for SMH and daughters, a partnership of florists. The partners are Sally Harris and her daughter Charlotte. The partnership profits are divided equally between Sally and Charlotte. The partnership makes up accounts to 31 December each year.

The following information relates to the year to 31 December 2020:

	£
Revenue	96,000
Cost of flowers sold	35,000
Allowable expenses	22,000
Capital allowances	4,500

Use this information to complete page 6 of the partnership tax return for Sally Harris.

Partnership Statement (short) for the year ended 5 April 2021

Please read these instructions before completing the Statement

Use these pages to allocate partnership income if the only income for the relevant return period was trading and professional income or untaxed interest and alternative finance receipts from UK banks and building societies. Otherwise you must download the 'Partnership Statement (Full)' pages to record details of the allocation of all the partnership income. Go to www.gov.uk/taxreturnforms

Step 1 Fill in boxes 1 to 29 and boxes A and B as appropriate. Get the figures you need from the relevant boxes in the Partnership Tax Return. Complete a separate Statement for each accounting period covered by this Partnership Tax Return and for each trade or profession carried on by the partnership.

Step 2 Then allocate the amounts in boxes 11 to 29 attributable to each partner using the allocation columns on this page and page 7, read the Partnership Tax Return Guide, go to www.gov.uk/taxreturnforms
If the partnership has more than 3 partners, please photocopy page 7.

Step 3 Each partner will need a copy of their allocation of income to fill in their personal tax return.

PARTNERSHIP INFORMATION
If the partnership business includes a trade or profession, enter here the accounting period for which appropriate items in this statement are returned.

Start **1** / /

End **2** / /

Nature of trade **3**

MIXED PARTNERSHIPS

Tick here if this Statement is drawn up using Corporation Tax rules **4**   Tick here if this Statement is drawn up using tax rules for non-residents **5**

Individual partner details

6 Name of partner
Address
Postcode

Date appointed as a partner (if during 2019-20 or 2020-21) Partner's Unique Taxpayer Reference (UTR)
7 / /   **8**

Date ceased to be a partner (if during 2019-20 or 2020-21) Partner's National Insurance number
9 / /   **10**

Partnership's profits, losses, income and tax credits

Tick this box if the items entered in the box had foreign tax taken off

Partner's share of profits, losses, income and tax credits

Copy figures in boxes 11 to 29 to boxes in the individual's Partnership (short) pages as shown below

- for an accounting period ended in 2020/21 ▼

from box 3.83	Profit from a trade or profession **A**	**11** £	Profit **11** £	Copy this figure to box 8
from box 3.82	Adjustment on change of basis	**11A** £	**11A** £	Copy this figure to box 10
from box 3.84	Loss from a trade or profession **B**	**12** £	Loss **12** £	Copy this figure to box 8
from box 3.94	Disguised remuneration	**12A**	**12A**	Copy to box 15

- for the period 6 April 2020 to 5 April 2021*

from box 7.9A	Income from untaxed UK savings	**13** £	**13** £	Copy this figure to box 28
from box 3.97	CIS deductions made by contractors on account of tax	**24** £	**24** £	Copy this figure to box 30
from box 3.98	Other tax taken off trading income	**24A** £	**24A** £	Copy this figure to box 31
from box 3.117	Partnership charges	**29** £	**29** £	Copy this figure to box 4, 'Other tax reliefs' section on page Ai 2 in your personal tax return

* If you're a 'CT Partnership' see the Partnership Tax Return Guide

SA800 2021   PARTNERSHIP TAX RETURN: PAGE 6

(Adapted from HMRC, 2020)

Task 5

K Ltd decides to make up accounts for a 15 month period of account to 30 November 2020. Trading profits were £10,000 per month for the first 10 months and £12,000 per month thereafter. It made a capital gain of £10,000 in January 2020 and a capital gain of £20,000 in October 2020.

Identify whether the following statements are true or false.

	True ✓	False ✓
The gain of £10,000 will be dealt with in the accounting period to 31 August 2020 and the gain of £20,000 will be dealt with in the accounting period to 30 November 2020.		
Trading profits will be £124,000 in the accounting period to 31 August 2020 and £36,000 in the accounting period to 30 November 2020.		

Task 6

Abdul is in business as a sole trader. His taxable trading profits for 2020/21 are £56,000, and he receives dividends of £9,000 in July 2020.

The Class 2 NIC liability for 2020/21 is:

£ [   ] . [ ]

The Class 4 NIC liability for 2020/21 is:

£ [   ] . [ ]

The total NIC liability for 2020/21 is:

£ [   ] . [ ]

Task 7

SR plc makes up accounts to 31 October each year. It is not a large company.

The corporation tax liability of SR plc for the year to 31 October 2020 was £24,000 and for the year to 31 October 2021 was £36,000.

(a) **How will SR plc pay the corporation tax liability for the year to 31 October 2021?**

	✓
Four instalments of £6,000 each due on 14 May 2021, 14 August 2021, 14 November 2021 and 14 February 2022 with a balancing payment of £12,000 due on 14 April 2022	
One payment due on 31 January 2023	
Four instalments of £9,000 each due on 14 May 2021, 14 August 2021, 14 November 2021 and 14 February 2022	
One payment due on 1 August 2022	

(b) **Tick the appropriate box for each of the following statements.**

	True ✓	False ✓
The maximum penalty for an error in a tax return which is deliberate but not concealed is 75%.		
If an individual submits his 2020/21 tax return online on 13 January 2022, HMRC can start an enquiry at any time before 31 January 2023.		
If a company submits its tax return two months late, the penalty is £100.		

Task 8

Osian makes a trading loss of £5,000 in 2020/21. He has property income of £6,300 in 2020/21. Osian had taxable trading income of £15,000 in 2019/20 and property income of £2,000.

(a) **Identify whether the following statements are true or false.**

	True ✓	False ✓
Osian can claim to use his loss of 2020/21 against his general income in 2019/20 only, in order to preserve his personal allowance in 2020/21.		
Osian can claim to use his loss of 2020/21 against his trading income in 2019/20 only, in order to preserve his personal allowance in 2020/21.		
Osian must claim to use his loss of 2020/21 against his general income in 2020/21, before being able to carry it back.		

(b) **Identify whether the following statements are true or false for a company.**

	True ✓	False ✓
When a trading loss is carried back by a company, it is set-off after deducting qualifying charitable donations.		
A company can carry a trade loss back 12 months against total profits and forward 36 months against profits of the same trade.		
A company must set-off trading losses in the current period before carrying back to the previous period.		

Task 9

(a) **Which TWO of the following are not fundamental principles of professional ethics?**

	✓
Confidentiality	
Professional intellect	
Integrity	
Courtesy and consideration	
Professional competence and due care	

(b) **State whether each of the following actions by a taxpayer would constitute tax evasion?**

	Tax evasion	Not tax evasion
Earning tax-free dividends in an ISA		
Deciding not to declare trading income earned		
Failing to notify HMRC of starting to earn rental income		
Claiming capital allowances on a non-existent piece of plant or machinery		

Task 10

Ros bought 2,000 shares in Blueberry Ltd for £10,000 in November 2007.

In March 2009, she received 400 shares in a bonus issue. In May 2011 the company offered a rights issue at 1 share for every 6 held. She accepted this rights issue at £3 per share. She sold 1,800 shares in Blueberry Ltd in July 2020 for £13,500.

Using the proforma layouts provided, show the chargeable gain on sale.

Share pool

	No of shares	Cost £

Gain

	£
Proceeds of sale	
Less allowable cost	
Chargeable gain	

Task 11

Three taxpayers sold similar assets during 2020/21 and each made a capital gain, after deducting their annual exempt amount, of £21,000. In the table below, the total of their other taxable income is shown.

The basic rate band for 2020/21 is £37,500.

Show the amount of capital gain that would be chargeable under each of the two rates of capital gains tax (CGT). You must enter 0 if your answer is zero.

		Chargeable capital gain £	
Taxpayer	Other taxable income £	10% CGT rate	20% CGT rate
Peter	11,300		
Richard	26,100		
Gemma	66,800		

BPP PRACTICE ASSESSMENT 4
BUSINESS TAX

ANSWERS

Business Tax (BSTX)
BPP practice assessment 4

Task 1

Jeremy Ltd adjusted trading profit for the year ending 31 March 2021

	£	£
Profit for the year per accounts		82,290
	Add	Deduct
Profit on sale of shares	0	13,550
Dividends received	0	6,300
Interest income	0	4,500
Qualifying charitable donation	500	0
Entertaining customers	9,550	0
Entertaining staff	0	0
Parking fines incurred by director	610	0
Petrol used by director for private use	0	0
Leasing costs of car for director (£9,300 × 15%)	1,395	0
Wages and salaries	0	0
Administrative expenses	0	0
Depreciation charge	15,700	0
Capital allowances	0	8,750
Total to add/deduct	27,755	33,100
Taxable trading profit		76,945

Task 2

(a)

	Total £	Xavier £	Yvonne £	Zebedee £
Period to 31/12/2020				
Salary (× 3/12)	2,250	2,250	0	0
Share of profits (2:2:1)	50,000	20,000	20,000	10,000
Period to 30/09/2021				
Share of profits (2:1)	156,750	0	104,500	52,250
Total profit for y/e 30/09/2021	209,000	22,250	124,500	62,250

(b) Xavier's taxable partnership profits for the tax year of cessation are:

£	38,750

Workings

2020/21	£
Profit for y/e 30 September 2020	21,000
Profit for p/e 31 December 2020	22,250
Less overlap profit	(4,500)
Taxable profit for 2020/21	38,750

Task 3

Year ended 31 January 2021

	AIA £	Main pool £	Car (20% business) £	Allowances £
B/f		58,060		
AIA additions				
June 2020	900,000			
December 2020	204,250			
	1,104,250			
AIA See note)	(933,333)			933,333
Transfer to main pool	(170,917)	170,917		
Disposals		(23,900)		
Non-AIA addition				
Car			19,320	
		205,077		
WDA @ 18%		(36,914)		36,914
WDA @ 18%			(3,478) × 20%	696
		168,163	15,842	970,943

Note. The limit of the AIA reduced from £1,000,000 to £200,000 from 01/01/2021. The maximum AIA is (11/12 × 1,000,000) + (1/12 × 200,000) =933,333

Task 4

Partnership tax adjusted trading profit £(96,000 − 35,000 − 22,000 − 4,500) = £34,500

Page 6

Box 1	01.01.20
Box 2	31.12.20
Box 3	Florists
Box 11	£34,500
Box 6	Sally Harris
Box 11 (in right hand column)	£17,250

Task 5

	True ✓	False ✓
The gain of £10,000 will be dealt with in the accounting period to 31 August 2020 and the gain of £20,000 will be dealt with in the accounting period to 30 November 2020.	✓	
Trading profits will be £124,000 in the accounting period to 31 August 2020 and £36,000 in the accounting period to 30 November 2020.		✓

Trading profits will be £128,000 in the accounting period to 31 August 2020 and £32,000 in the accounting period to 30 November 2020, as they are deemed to accrue evenly.

Task 6

The Class 2 NIC liability for 2020/21 is:

£	158	.	60

Working

(£3.05 × 52)

The Class 4 NIC liability for 2020/21 is:

£	3,765	.	00

Working

£(50,000 − 9,500) × 9% + £(56,000 − 50,000) × 2%

The total NIC liability for 2020/21 is:

£	3,923	.	60

Task 7

(a)

	✓
Four instalments of £6,000 each due on 14 May 2021, 14 August 2021, 14 November 2021 and 14 February 2022 with a balancing payment of £12,000 due on 14 April 2022	
One payment due on 31 January 2023	
Four instalments of £9,000 each due on 14 May 2021, 14 August 2021, 14 November 2021 and 14 February 2022	
One payment due on 1 August 2022	✓

(b)

	True ✓	False ✓
The maximum penalty for an error in a tax return which is deliberate but not concealed is 75%.		✓ (70%)
If an individual submits his 2020/21 tax return online on 13 January 2022, HMRC can start an enquiry at any time before 31 January 2023.		✓ (return submitted by due date: one year from actual filing date)
If a company submits its tax return two months late, the penalty is £100.	✓	

Task 8

(a)

	True ✓	False ✓
Osian can claim to use his loss of 2020/21 against his general income in 2019/20 only, in order to preserve his personal allowance in 2020/21.	✓	
Osian can claim to use his loss of 2020/21 against his trading income in 2019/20 only, in order to preserve his personal allowance in 2020/21.		✓
Osian must claim to use his loss of 2020/21 against his general income in 2020/21, before being able to carry it back.		✓

(b)

	True ✓	False ✓
When a trading loss is carried back by a company, it is set-off after deducting qualifying charitable donations.		✓
A company can carry a trading loss back 12 months against total profits and forward 36 months against profits of the same trade.		✓
A company must set-off trading losses in the current period before carrying back to the previous period.	✓	

When a trading loss is carried back by a company, it is set-off before deducting qualifying charitable donations.

When trade losses are carried forward there is no restriction, they are carried forward indefinitely, against total profits.

Task 9

(a)

	✓
Confidentiality	
Professional intellect	✓
Integrity	
Courtesy and consideration	✓
Professional competence and due care	

'Professional intellect' and Courtesy and consideration' would be required of a professional accountant but are not of themselves fundamental principles.

(b)

	Tax evasion	Not tax evasion
Earning tax-free dividends in an ISA		✓
Deciding not to declare trading income earned	✓	
Failing to notify HMRC of starting to earn rental income	✓	
Claiming capital allowances on a non-existent piece of plant or machinery	✓	

Earning tax free dividends in an ISA is a legitimate way to reduce tax.

Task 10

Share pool

	No. of shares	Cost £
November 2007 Acquisition	2,000	10,000
March 2009 Bonus	400	Nil
	2,400	10,000
May 2011 Rights 1 for 6 @ £3	400	1,200
	2,800	11,200
July 2020 Disposal	(1,800)	(7,200)
c/f	1000	4,000

Gain

	£
Proceeds of sale	13,500
Less allowable cost	(7,200)
Chargeable gain	6,300

Task 11

Taxpayer	Other taxable income £	Chargeable capital gain £	
		10% CGT rate	20% CGT rate
Peter	11,300	21,000	0
Richard	26,100	11,400	9,600
Gemma	66,800	0	21,000

1 Taxation tables for business tax – 2020/21

1.1 Capital allowances

Annual investment allowance
Prior to 1 January 2019	£200,000
Between 1 January 2019 and 31 December 2020	£1,000,000
From 1 January 2021	£200,000

Plant and machinery writing down allowance
Assets other than motor cars	18%

Motor cars
CO_2 emissions up to 50 g/km	100%
CO_2 emissions between 51 and 110 g/km	18%
CO_2 emissions over 110 g/km – Prior to 1 April 2019/6 April 2019	8%
CO_2 emissions over 110 g/km – From 1 April 2019/6 April 2019	6%

1.2 Capital gains

Annual exempt amount	£12,300
Basic rate	10%
Higher rate	20%
Business asset disposal relief rate	10%
Investors' relief rate	10%
Business asset disposal relief lifetime allowance	£1,000,000
Investors' relief lifetime allowance	£10,000,000

1.3 National Insurance rates

Class 2 contributions:	£3.05 per week
Small profits threshold	£6,475p.a.

Class 4 contributions:
Main rate	9%
Additional rate	2%
Lower profits limit	£9,500
Upper profits limit	£50,000

1.4 Trading allowance

This allowance is available to individuals only.   £1,000

1.5 Corporation tax

Financial year	**2020**	**2019**
All profits and gains	19%	19%

2 Introduction to business tax

2.1 Administration

- Taxation administered by HM Revenue & Customs (HMRC).

- Rules covering tax are contained in statute (law) which is passed every year (*Finance Act*).

- Decisions reached by the courts interpreting the law are known as case law.

- HMRC also issue guidance – Extra Statutory Concessions and Statements of Practice.

2.2 Taxes

- Corporation Tax – paid by companies on both income and chargeable gains.

- Income Tax – paid by individuals on their income.

- Capital Gains Tax – paid by individuals on their capital gains.

2.3 Tax evasion, tax avoidance and tax planning

- Tax evasion: any action taken to evade tax by illegal means; this carries a risk of criminal prosecution. Examples of tax evasion include failing to declare income and claiming false expenses.

- Tax avoidance: bending the rules of the tax system to gain a tax advantage that Parliament never intended. It involves operating within the letter of the law but not the spirit of the law.

- Tax planning: use of legitimate means to minimise taxpayer's tax liability, for example by investing in a tax-free ISA (Individual Savings Account).

3 Adjustment of profits – sole traders, partnerships and companies

3.1 Pro forma for adjustment of profits

	£	£
Net profit as per accounts		X
Add: Expenses charged in the accounts that are not allowable as trading expenses	X	
		X
		X
Less: Income included in the accounts which is not assessable as trading income	X	
		(X)
Adjusted profit/(loss)		X

3.2 Disallowed expenses

- Expenses that fail the remoteness test so not "wholly and exclusively" for trading purposes.

- Fines on the business or fraud by directors/owners.

- Donations to charity are generally disallowed in calculating trading profits (however qualifying charitable donations are deductible in the corporation tax computation).

- Political donations are never allowable.

- Capital expenditure e.g. purchase of equipment included in profit and loss account.

- Depreciation. Capital allowances granted instead.

- Costs of bringing newly acquired second-hand assets to useable condition.

- Legal and professional expenses relating to capital items or breaking the law.

- Customer entertaining. Staff entertaining can be allowable.

- Customer gifts, unless gift incorporates business advertising, cost is less than £50 per annum per customer, and gift is not food, drink, tobacco or cash vouchers.

3.3 Non-assessable income

- Income taxed in any other way, e.g. interest or property income for individuals.

- Profits on sale of fixed assets.

4 Unincorporated businesses – trading income

4.1 Trading income calculated for each period of account:

	£
Adjusted accounting profit	X
Less: Capital allowances:	(X)
Less: Balancing allowances	(X)
Plus: Balancing charges	X
Trading income for the period of account	X

4.2 Expenses charged in the accounts which are not allowable as trading expenses

- See adjustment of profits – sole traders, partnerships and companies.

- Transactions with the owner of the business. For example:

   – Add back salary paid to owner. Salaries paid to family members do not need to be added back.

   – Private expenditure included in accounts.

   – Class 2 and Class 4 National Insurance contributions.

   – Goods taken for own use.

5 Sole traders – basis periods

Tax year – 2020/21 tax year runs from 6 April 2020 to 5 April 2021.

5.1 Basis period rules

- First year – runs from start date of trading to the next 5 April.
- Second year and third year.

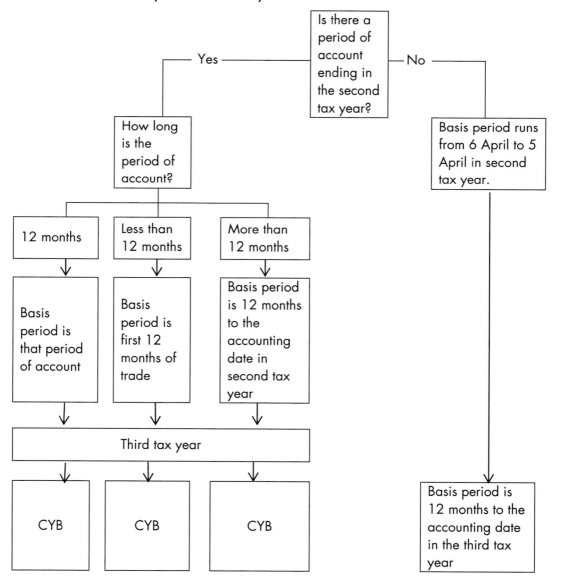

Later years – basis period is the period of account ending in the tax year = Current Year basis (CYB).

Final year – basis period is the period from the end of the basis period for the previous tax year to cessation date.

Overlap profits – opening year rules may lead to profits being taxed twice. Relief is given on cessation of the business.

6 Sole traders – change of accounting date

For an accounting date change to be recognised for tax purposes the following conditions must be satisfied:

- the first accounts ending on the new date must not exceed 18 months in length

- the sole trader or partnership must give notice of the change in the tax return by the filing date of the tax return

- the change will not be permitted if there has been a change of accounting date in the previous five years unless there are genuine commercial reasons for the change.

Steps:

Step 1: Identify the year of change. This is the first year when current year basis is not possible.

Step 2: For all years before the year of change, the basis period is the 12 months to the old year end date.

Step 3: For all years after the year of change, the basis period is the 12 months to the new year end date.

Step 4: In the year of change, identify the relevant period'. The relevant period is the time to the new accounting date from the end of the previous basis period (example: all profits which have not been assessed as a result of steps 2 and 3)

- If the relevant period > 12 months, tax the profits of the relevant period but deduct overlap profits from commencement such that 12 months in total are taxed. The basis period is the same as the relevant period.

- If the relevant period is < 12 months, tax the 12 month period to the end of the relevant period (this will mean taxing some profits from the previous period twice, creating additional overlap profits). The basis period is the 12 months to the end of the relevant period.

6.1 Example 1 – relevant period is less than 12 months

Jasmin changes her accounting date as follows:

Accounts	Year	Period
Year to 31 December 2019	2019/20	1/1/19 to 31/12/19
Nine months to 30 September 2020	2020/21	1/10/19 to 30/9/20
Year to 30 September 2021	2021/22	1/10/20 to 30/9/21

Year of change – 2020/21

Relevant period – nine months to 30 September 2020

Basis period for 20/21 – 12 months to 30 September 2020

6.2 Example 2 – relevant period is greater than 12 months

Vaughan changes his accounting date as follows:

Accounts	Year	Period
Year to 31 December 2019	2019/20	1/1/19 to 31/12/19
15 months to 31 March 2021	2020/21	1/1/20 to 31/3/21
Year to 31 March 2022	2021/22	1/4/21 to 31/3/22

Year of change – 2020/21

Relevant period – 15 months to 31 March 2021

Basis period for 20/21 – 15 months to 31 March 2021

7 Capital allowances on plant and machinery

7.1 Layout of capital allowances on plant and machinery computation

(see taxation tables for rates)

	First Year Allowance (FYA) £	Annual Investment Allowance (AIA) £	General pool £	Special rate pool £	Short Life Asset £	Total allowances £
WDV b/f			X	X	X	
Additions	X	X	X			
Disposals	—	—	(X)	—	(X)	
	X	X	X	X	X	
Balancing allowance/balancing charge (BA/BC)					X/(X)	X/(X)
					Nil	
AIA/FYA	(X)	(X)				X
Writing down allowance @ 18% pa			(X)			X
Writing down allowance @ X% pa	—	—	—	(X)		X
WDV c/f	Nil	Nil	X	X		—
Total allowances						X

- Plant – defined by 'function/setting' distinction and case law.

- AIA – 100% allowance for expenditure (other than cars) in 12-month period (pro rata). Expenditure in excess of AIA qualifies for writing down allowance (WDA). If the accounting period straddles 1 January 2019 or 1 January 2021, the AIA must be pro-rated.

- Full WDA for the period is given regardless of date of purchase of item. WDA is scaled for periods other than 12 months.

- The WDA % on the special rate pool is calculated as: ((8 × number of months before 1 April 2019) + (6 × number of months after 1 April 2019))/number of months in the chargeable period. This % should be rounded to two decimal places.

- FYA – 100% allowance given on purchase of low CO_2 emission cars. FYA is not scaled for short accounting periods.

- If the written down value (WDV) on the general pool (= WDV b/f + additions-disposals) is £1,000 or less then an election can be made to write off the pool balance, known as a 'small pools allowance'.

- Short life assets (SLA) – de-pool asset if life expected to be less than 8 years. Not available for cars.

7.2 Unincorporated businesses – Private use assets

- Private use assets have separate column in Capital Allowance computation.

- Disallow private use % of WDA/AIA/FYA.

7.3 Capital allowances – business cessation

- In the cessation period of account, no WDA/AIA/FYA.

- Include additions and disposals as normal. Any asset taken over by owner, treat as a disposal at market value. Balancing adjustment made (balancing charge or balancing allowance).

8 Partnerships

- Each partner is taxed like a sole trader on their share of the partnership profits.

- First step is to share accounting profits between partners:
  - allocate the correct salaries and interest on capital for the period to each partner
  - divide the remaining profit for each set of accounts between the partners based upon the profit sharing arrangement
  - you may need to split the period if there is a change such as a partner joining or leaving.

- Opening year and cessation rules apply to partners individually when they join or leave the partnership.

- Allocate the profit for each partner to the correct tax year using usual basis period rules.

- Basis periods for continuing partners are unaffected by joiners or leavers.

- Each partner enters their share of profits for a tax year in the partnership pages of their own tax return.

9 Trading losses for sole traders and partners

9.1 Trading losses for sole traders and partners

- A loss is computed in the same way as a profit, making the same adjustments to the net profit as per the accounts and deducting capital allowances.

9.2 Set off of trading loss against total income

- Set off loss against total income of the preceding tax year and/or the tax year of loss, e.g. loss in 2020/21 set off against total income in 2019/20 and/or 2020/21.

- Cannot restrict loss to preserve use of personal allowance so personal allowance may be wasted.

- For 2020/21 loss claim needed by 31 January 2023.

9.3 Carry forward of trading losses

- If any loss remains unrelieved after current year and carry back claim has been made, or no such claims are made, then carry forward the loss against first available profits of the same trade.

9.4 Choice of loss relief – consider the following:

- utilise loss in the tax year in which income is taxed at a higher rate

- possible wastage of personal allowance

- review the projected future profits to ensure the loss can be utilised

- if cash flow is important, a loss carry back claim may result in a tax refund being paid to the business.

10 Payment and administration – sole traders and partners

10.1 The return must be filed by:

- 31 October following the end of the tax year if filing a paper return
- 31 January following the end of the tax year if filing online.

10.2 Penalties for late filing and payment

Late filing	Late payment	Penalty
Miss filing deadline		£100
	30 days late	5% of tax outstanding at that date
3 months late		Daily penalty £10 per day for up to 90 days (max £900)
6 months late		5% of tax due or £300, if greater
	6 months late	5% of tax outstanding at that date
12 months late		5% of tax due or £300, if greater
	12 months late	5% of tax outstanding at that date
12 months and information deliberately withheld		Based on behaviour: • deliberate and concealed withholding 100% of tax due, or • £300 if greater. • deliberate but not concealed 70% of tax due, or £300 if greater. Reductions apply for prompted and unprompted disclosures and for cooperation with investigation.

10.3 Disclosure and errors

- Taxpayer must notify HMRC by 5 October following end of the tax year if a tax return is needed.

- Taxpayer can amend a tax return within 12 months of filing date or make a claim for overpayment relief within four years of the end of the tax year.

10.4 Payments on account (POA)

- Due 31 January (in tax year) and 31 July (after tax year end). Each instalment is 50% of the previous year's tax and Class 4 National Insurance contribution (NIC) liability after taking into account any tax deducted at source.

- Balancing payment made 31 January after tax year end.

- No POA due if:

  - last year's tax and Class 4 NIC liability is less than £1,000 or
  - if greater than 80% of last year's liability was deducted at source.

- Can reduce this year's POA if this year's liability expected to be less than last year's. Penalties and interest will be charged if a deliberate incorrect claim is made.

- Capital gains tax (CGT) liability and Class 2 National Insurance is paid 31 January following the tax year end. No POA needed for CGT and Class 2 National Insurance.

10.5 Interest on tax paid late/overpaid tax

- Interest charged daily on late payment.

11 Enquiries and other penalties

- HMRC must notify individual of enquiry within 12 months of submission of return.

- Basis of enquiry – random or HMRC believe income/expenses misstated.

- Penalty for failure to produce enquiry documents = £300 + £60 per day.

- Penalty for failure to keep proper records is up to £3,000. Records must be kept for five years after the filing date for the relevant tax year.

- Penalties for incorrect returns are detailed in the table below:

Type of behaviour	Maximum	Unprompted (minimum)	Prompted (minimum)
Genuine mistake: despite taking reasonable care	0%	0%	0%
Careless error and inaccuracy are due to failure to take reasonable care	30%	0%	15%
Deliberate error but not concealed	70%	20%	35%
Deliberate error and concealed	100%	30%	50%

12 National Insurance contributions

- Self-employed individuals pay Class 2 and Class 4 contributions.

- Class 4 contributions are at 9% on profits between the lower and upper limits, then 2% on profits above the upper limit.

- Percentages and limits are provided in the Taxation Tables.

13 An outline of corporation tax

- Companies pay corporation tax on their profits for each accounting period.

- There is one rate of corporation tax set each financial year.

- Profits = Income + Gains − Qualifying charitable donations

- Accounting periods are usually 12 months long but can be shorter.

- If a company's accounts are longer than 12 months, the first 12 months will be one accounting period and the remainder a second accounting period.

- All UK property income is pooled as a single source of income and taxed on an accruals basis.

- Borrowing or lending money by a company is a loan relationship.

- Trading loan relationships are part of trading income.

- Non-trading loan relationships (NTL-R) are pooled to give NTL-R credits or deficits.

- Donations to charities are qualifying charitable donations.

- Company A is a related 51% group company of company B if:
  - A is a 51% subsidiary of B, or
  - B is a 51% subsidiary of A, or
  - A and B are both 51% subsidiaries of the same company.

'A' is a 51% subsidiary of 'B' if more than 50% of its ordinary share capital is beneficially owned (directly or indirectly) by 'B'.

14 The calculation of total profits and corporation tax payable

ABC Ltd

Corporation tax computation for the year/period ended DD/MM/20XX

	£
Trading income – accruals basis	X
Interest income (NTL-R) – accrual basis	X
Property income – accruals basis	X
Chargeable gains	X
	X
Less Qualifying charitable donations	(X)
Total taxable profits	X
Corporation tax payable – Total taxable profits × Corporation tax rate	X

14.1 Key points

- Trading income is adjusted from net profit per company accounts less capital allowances.

- Companies receive interest gross.

- Virtually all interest receivable is taxed as interest income (NTL-R).

- Dividends payable by a company are not an allowable expense.

- UK dividends receivable by a company are not taxable.

- Net-off current year capital losses against current year capital gains. If there is a net capital loss carry it forward.

- See taxation tables for corporation tax rates.

14.2 Long periods of account

- Will consist of two accounting periods = first 12 months and remainder of period.

- Split profits as follows:

- Adjusted trading profit – time apportion.

- Capital allowances – separate computations for each accounting period.

- Interest income (NTL-R) and property income – accruals basis.

- Chargeable gains – according to date of disposal.

- Qualifying charitable donations– according to date paid.

15 Corporation tax – trade losses

- Can elect to set trading losses against current accounting period 'total profits'. Qualifying charitable donations will remain unrelieved.

- If the above election is made, can also carry back trading loss to set against 'total profits' within the previous 12 months.

- Losses not relieved in the current accounting period or previous 12 months are carried forward and an election can be made to set against total profits in future periods.

- If there is a choice of loss relief, firstly consider when the loss was incurred, the rate of loss relief and then the timing of relief.

- Set out the use of the losses in a loss memorandum.

16 Corporation tax – payment and administration

16.1 Payment dates

- Small companies (annual profits less than £1.5 million): nine months + 1 day after end of the accounting period (AP).

- Large companies (annual profits greater than £1.5 million) must estimate year's tax liability and pay 25% of the year's liability:
    - six months and 14 days after start of AP
    - nine months and 14 days after start of AP
    - 14 days after end of AP
    - three months and 14 days after end of AP.

- Estimate must be revised for each quarter. Penalties may be charged if company deliberately fails to pay sufficient instalments.

- No instalments due for first year company is large unless profits are greater than £10 million.

- 51% group companies share the annual profit limit of £1.5 million equally.

16.2 Interest on late payments

- Interest charged daily on late payment. Overpayment of tax receives interest from HMRC. Interest is taxable/tax allowable as interest income.

16.3 Filing the return

- Filed on the later of 12 months after end of AP or three months after the notice to deliver a tax return has been issued.

- Late filing penalties are: less than three months late: £100; greater than three months late: £200; greater than six months late: 10% of tax due per return; greater than 12 months late: 20% of tax due per return.

- Company must notify HMRC it is within scope of corporation tax within 3 months of starting to trade.

- Company can amend return within 12 months of the filing date.

16.4 Enquiries and other penalties

- HMRC must notify company of enquiry within 12 months of submission of return.

- Basis of enquiry – random or HMRC believe income/expenses misstated.

- Penalty for failure to produce enquiry documents: £300 + £60 per day.

- Penalty for failure to keep proper records is up to £3,000. Records must be retained for six years after the end of the relevant accounting period.

- Penalties for incorrect returns are the same as for sole traders and partners – see sole traders and partners link.

- Penalties for incorrect returns are the same as for sole traders and partners – see sole traders and partners link.

17 Current tax reliefs and other tax issues

17.1 Research and development (R&D) tax credits for small and medium sized companies

A small or medium sized enterprise (SME) is a company with less than 500 employees with either:

- an annual turnover under €100 million, or
- a balance sheet under €86 million.

17.2 The SME tax relief scheme

The tax relief on allowable R&D costs is 230%.

17.3 R&D tax credits

If a company makes a loss, it can choose to receive R&D tax credits instead of carrying forward a loss.

17.4 Costs that qualify for R&D tax relief

To qualify as R&D, any activity must contribute directly to seeking an advance in science or technology or must be a qualifying indirect activity. The costs must relate to the company's trade – either an existing one, or one that they intend to start up based on the results of the R&D.

17.5 Intermediaries (IR35) legislation

IR35 legislation prevents personal service companies ("PSC") being used to disguise permanent employment.

The rules apply where the relationship between the worker and the client, would be considered to be an employment relationship if the existence of the PSC was ignored.

If the rules apply, a **deemed employment income tax charge** is charged on the PSC.

The **deemed employment income tax charge** is calculated based upon the actual payments made to the PSC by the client.

18 Introduction to capital/chargeable gains

- Individual pays Capital Gains Tax (CGT) on net chargeable gains in a tax year.

- For companies, chargeable gains are included as income in calculating total profits.

- Individuals receive an annual exempt amount from CGT – for 2020/21 this is £12,300.

- Gains/losses arise when a chargeable person makes a chargeable disposal of a chargeable asset.

- Chargeable person – individual or company.

- Chargeable disposal – sale, gift or loss/destruction of the whole or part of an asset. Exempt disposals – on death and gifts to approved charities.

- Chargeable asset – all assets unless exempt. Exempt assets include motor cars and some chattels.

18.1 Calculation of capital gains tax

Net chargeable gains – total gains in the tax year after netting off any current year or brought forward losses and the annual exempt amount.

18.2 Annual exempt amount (AEA)

- For individuals only.

- AEA cannot be carried forward or carried back.

- Current year losses must be netted off against current year gains before AEA. This means AEA can be wasted.

- Brought forward capital losses are set off against current year gains after AEA so AEA is not wasted.

19 Calculation of gains and losses for individuals

19.1 Pro forma computation

	£	£
Consideration received		X
Less Incidental costs of sale		(X)
Net sale proceeds		NSP
Less Allowable expenditure		
– Acquisition cost	X	
– Incidental costs of acquisition	X	
– Enhancement expenditure	X	
		(Cost)
Gain/(Loss)		X/(X)

- Consideration received is usually sales proceeds, but market value will be used instead of actual consideration where the transaction is a gift or between connected persons.

- An individual is connected with their spouse, relatives (and their spouses) and spouse's relatives (and their spouses). Relative means brother, sister, lineal ancestor or lineal descendent.

- Husband and wife/civil partner transfers – nil gain nil loss.

Part disposals – the cost allocated to the disposal = Cost × (A/(A + B))

A = consideration received on part disposal

B = market value of the remainder of the asset

Chattels – tangible moveable object.

Two types:

- Wasting – expected life of 50 years or less (e.g. racehorse or boat). CGT exempt.

- Non-wasting – expected life greater than 50 years (e.g. antiques or jewellery).

19.2 CGT, £6,000 rule

Buy / Sell	£6,000 or less	More than £6,000
Less than £6,000	Exempt	Allowable loss but proceeds are deemed = £6,000
More than £6,000	Normal calculation of the gain, then compare with 5/3 (gross proceeds – £6,000) – Take the lower gain	Chargeable in full

20 Shares and securities – disposals by individuals

20.1 CGT on shares and securities

Disposal of shares and securities are subject to CGT except for listed government securities (gilt-edged securities or 'gilts'), qualifying corporate bonds (e.g. company loan notes/debentures) and shares held in an Individual Savings Account (ISA).

20.2 The identification rules

Used to determine which shares have been sold and so what acquisition cost can be deducted from the sale proceeds (e.g. match the disposal and acquisition).

Disposals are matched:

- firstly, with acquisitions on the same day as the day of disposal

- secondly, with acquisitions made in the 30 days following the date of disposal (FIFO basis)

- thirdly, with shares from the share pool.

20.3 The Share Pool

- The share pool contains all shares acquired prior to the disposal date.

- Each acquisition is not kept separately, but is 'pooled' together with other acquisitions and a running total kept of the number of shares and the cost of those shares.

- When a disposal from the pool is made, the appropriate number of shares are taken from the pool along with the average cost of those shares.

- The gain on disposal is then calculated.

20.4 Bonus issues and rights issues

- Bonus issue – no adjustment to cost needed.
- Rights issue – adjustment to cost needed.

21 Chargeable gains – reliefs available to individuals

Replacement of business assets (Rollover) relief – when a qualifying business asset is sold at a gain, taxpayer can defer gain by reinvesting proceeds in a qualifying replacement asset.

- Deferred gain is deducted from the cost of the replacement asset so gain crystallises when the replacement asset is sold.

- Qualifying assets (original and replacement) – must be used in a trade by the vendor and be land and buildings, fixed plant and machinery or goodwill.

- Qualifying time period – replacement asset must be purchased between 1 year before and 3 years after the sale of the original asset.

- Partial reinvestment – only some of the sales proceeds reinvested then the gain taxable is the lower of the full gain and the proceeds not reinvested.

Gift relief (holdover relief) – donee takes over asset at donor's base cost i.e. the gain is given away along with the asset.

- Qualifying assets – trade assets of donor or shares in any unquoted trading company or personal trading company (donor owns at least 5% of company).

Business asset disposal relief – gain taxable at 10% capital gains tax rate.

- The £1 million limit is a lifetime limit which is reduced each time a claim for the relief is made.

- For 2020/21 a claim must be made by 31 January 2023.

- Qualifying business disposals (assets must be owned for at least 24 months prior to sale).

  - The whole or part of a business carried on by the individual (alone or in partnership).

  - Assets of the individual's or partnership's trading business that has now ceased.

- Shares in the individual's 'personal trading company' where they have at least 5% of shares, voting rights, entitlement to distributable profits and entitlement to net assets. Individual must have owned the shares and been an employee of the company for 24 months prior to sale.

Investors relief – gain taxable at 10% capital gains tax rate

- The £10 million limit is a lifetime limit which is reduced each time a claim for the relief is made.

- For 2020/21 a claim must be made by 31 January 2023:
    - the individual subscribes for shares which are issued on or after 17 March 2016
    - the shares are ordinary shares
    - the issuing company is a trading company or holding company of a trading group
    - the shares are not listed on a recognised stock exchange
    - the individual has not been an officer or employee of the issuing company at any point during the ownership period
    - the shares are held continuously for three years.

22 Calculation of gains and losses for companies

22.1 Pro forma computation

	£	£
Consideration received		X
Less Incidental costs of sale		(X)
Net sale proceeds		NSP
Less Allowable expenditure		
Acquisition cost + incidental costs of acquisition	X	
Indexation allowance [indexation factor × expenditure]	X	
Enhancement expenditure	X	
Indexation allowance	X	
		(Cost)
Chargeable gain		Gain

- Companies are entitled to an indexation allowance, based on the changes in the retail price index (RPI) from the date when expenditure was incurred to the date of disposal (or deemed disposal).

- Indexation allowance is frozen at 31 December 2017.

- Disposals taking place from 1 January 2018 will use the RPI   at 31 December 2017 for indexation allowance purposes.

- Indexation allowance is not available where there is an unindexed loss; nor can it turn an unindexed gain into an indexed loss.

- Note that companies do not get an annual exempt amount.

- Losses relieved in order – current year first followed by losses brought forward.

22.2 Only relief available to companies is rollover relief:

- Rollover relief is a deferral relief – see Chargeable gains – reliefs available to individuals for main rollover relief rules.

- Key differences applying for companies:

    - indexation is given on disposal of the original asset.

    - goodwill is not a qualifying asset for companies.

    - gain deferred is the indexed gain.

    - on disposal of the replacement asset, indexation is calculated on the 'base cost' not actual cost.

23 Shares and securities – disposals by companies

The identification rules – a disposal of shares is matched:

- firstly, with same-day transactions

- secondly, with transactions in the previous nine days (FIFO). No indexation allowance is available.

- thirdly, with shares from the 1985 pool (shares bought from 1 April 1982 onwards).

1985 pool – pro forma working	**No.**	**Cost £**	**Indexed cost £**
Purchase	X	X	X
Index to next operative event			X̲
			X
Operative event (purchase)	X̲	X̲	X̲
	X	X	X
Index to next operative event			X̲
			X
Operative event (sale)	(X̲)	(X̲)	(X̲) A
Pool carried forward	X̲	X̲	X̲

Operative event = purchase, sale, rights issue. Bonus issue is not an operative event.

Computation

	£
Proceeds	X
Less indexed cost (A from pool)	(X̲)
Indexed gain	X̲

24 The badges of trade

- Profit seeking motive
- Number of transactions
- Nature of asset
- Existence of similar trading transactions or interests
- Changes to the asset
- The way the sale was carried out
- The source of finance
- Interval of time between purchase and sale
- Method of acquisition

25 Duties and responsibilities of a tax advisor

- Maintain client confidentiality at all times.

- AAT members must adopt an ethical approach and maintain an objective outlook.

- Give timely and constructive advice to clients.

- Honest and professional conduct with HMRC.

- A tax advisor is liable to a penalty if they assist in making an incorrect return.

These Reference Materials have been produced by the AAT